Hard Work Is Not Enough

Hard Work Is Not Enough

Gender and Racial Inequality in an Urban Workspace

Katrinell M. Davis

The University of North Carolina Press *Chapel Hill*

Cover illustration: © iStockphoto.com/DarioEgidi

The University of North Carolina Press has been a member of the Green Press
Initiative since 2003.

Library of Congress Cataloging-in-Publication Data

Names: Davis, Katrinell M., author.

Title: Hard work is not enough : gender and racial inequality in an urban
workspace / Katrinell M. Davis.

Description: Chapel Hill : University of North Carolina Press, [2016] |
Includes bibliographical references and index.

Identifiers: LCCN 2016008487 | ISBN 9781469630472 (cloth : alk. paper) |
ISBN 9781469630489 (pbk : alk. paper) | ISBN 9781469630496 (ebook)

Subjects: LCSH: Transport workers—California—Alameda County—Social
conditions. | Race discrimination—California—Alameda County. | Sex
discrimination against women—California—Alameda County. | African
American women—Employment—California—Alameda County. |
Work environment—California—Alameda County.

Classification: LCC HD8039.T72 U4425 2016 | DDC 331.13/30979465—dc23
LC record available at http://lccn.loc.gov/2016008487

*To the memory of the family members who transitioned
while I wrote this book, especially my mother,
DONELLA M. SWAN.
I love you.*

Contents

Tables

Acknowledgments

Over time, many have contributed to this book. I have been fortunate to meet people during my undergraduate and graduate years who have become long-term mentors and supporters of my work. Since my time as an undergraduate Social Relations major at James Madison College, a residential college at Michigan State University, Dr. Katherine O'Sullivan See has motivated and supported me. I am very grateful to have met such a kind and caring guide. From graduate school in the Department of Sociology at UC Berkeley to this day, I have benefited from the support of mentors who encouraged the development of my theoretical perspectives and my efforts to produce this analysis. I wish to thank the following people for choosing to support me throughout the years as well as those who played pivotal roles at crucial times throughout the journey of completing this manuscript: Drs. Margaret Weir, Sandra S. Smith, Michael Hout, Martin Sanchez-Jankowski, Barrie Thorne, and Steven Pitts. My home while in Berkeley eventually became the Institute for the Study of Social Change, now the Institute for the Study of Societal Issues. To my ISSC/ISSI family including David Minkus, Deborah Freedman Lustig, and Christine Trost, who guided me through some really tough times, thank you for being there to pull me out of my shell and to motivate me to produce sound scholarship, while maintaining an authentic voice and a commitment to social justice.

Much of the research and insight in this book was developed during my time as a Postdoctoral Fellow at the National Poverty Center at the University of Michigan between 2011 and 2013. In this space, I was able to sort through the archival data I gathered since 2008 and focus on this manuscript with excellent resources and mentors at my disposal. While a good share of my time was spent in local restaurants where hot coffee and decent snacks were available at a modest cost, I also had the privilege of joining workgroups within the University of Michigan where I felt supported and had the opportunity to present research and receive helpful feedback from seasoned and emerging scholars. Throughout my time as an NPC Postdoctoral Fellow, I have to thank the following people for their guidance, kindness, and support: Drs. Sheldon Danziger, Sandra

Danziger, Howard Kimeldorf, NPC staff and colleagues, in addition to my Emerging Scholars Interdisciplinary Network colleagues, including Drs. Sean Joe, Maria Johnson, Brandon Respress, and Ola Rostant. I also have to thank colleagues that I met through my participation in "write-ins" hosted by the Women of Color in the Academy Project, a campus-wide faculty network at the University of Michigan that is committed to promoting the work of women of color scholars.

My leave at the NPC was supported by the Joan Smith Faculty Research Support Award that I secured from the University of Vermont. I also benefited from the support of colleagues within the Department of Sociology at the University of Vermont as well as colleagues within this academic community who read segments of this manuscript and provided key insight and guidance. Big thanks to Drs. Beth Mintz, Elaine McCrate, and Stephanie Seguino for their help during crucial phases throughout this project.

While I had great guides and abundant support throughout the process of writing this book, this book would not exist if I hadn't met the women who chose to share their stories with me and who motivated me to take a closer look at their working conditions. I cannot be more thankful for their time, honesty, and kindness. I also wish to thank the archivists and staff at the following research centers, who helped me gather data: Labor Archives and Research Center at San Francisco State University; Tamiment Library and Robert F. Wagner Labor Archives at New York State University; the Bancroft Library and the Institute of Transportation Studies Library at the University of California, Berkeley; and the National Archives and Records Administration at San Francisco in San Bruno, California. I gained a great deal of support from their respective suggestions, research assistance, and professionalism. I am also grateful to have worked with copy editors Abigail Carroll and Letta Page, a great staff at the University of North Carolina Press, especially acquisitions editor, Joseph Parsons, as well as the readers who reviewed the manuscript and provided invaluable observations and suggestions.

Finally, I am thankful for the support I received from family and friends who supported me throughout this process. In particular, I thank my maternal grandparents for providing a compass and my mother, Donella M. Swan, for teaching me how to work hard and for moving to the East Bay for one year to watch my children while I was busy conducting interviews and analyzing data. I want to thank my cousins Joe and Lisa, for their hospitality throughout my stay as an NPC Fellow in Southeastern Michigan. To Dr. Libby Lewis, thank you for your valuable suggestions and persistent support. I appreciate your encouragement throughout this journey. To my kids, Kaitlyn and Elijah, thank you for your patience, kindness, and love. You guys motivate and challenge me to offer my best. And to Taj, my husband and partner of many years, who has supported and covered me through it all, thank you for being you and being there for me.

Katrinell M. Davis
Burlington, Vermont 2015

Hard Work Is Not Enough

Introduction

As a San Francisco Bay Area native, Mary grew up with Alameda–Contra Costa Transit District. While riding AC Transit buses to school, she often wondered what it would be like to operate the large buses and whether she could ever become a bus driver. In her late thirties, Mary, who once thought she was too petite for the job, overcame her fears and took the wheel. This was just under six years ago.

Like many East Bay area bus drivers, who prefer to be called "transit operators," Mary began as an operator for WestCAT, a small Bay Area transit company based in Pinole, California. The company and its entry level jobs help workers gain access to the experience needed to qualify for a better paying position with a large mass transit company. Mary worked for WestCAT a few years before she became aware of job positions with AC Transit. She was an ideal candidate. Unlike her friend, another applicant who had a recent accident on her work record, Mary knew the WestCAT routes, had a clean record, and had earned positive reviews of her work as a transit operator. WestCAT, however, paid very little and offered no opportunity for advancement, so she could not have been more thrilled to learn, after six to eight weeks of interviews and tests, that she had landed an AC Transit job.

Besides working as an AC transit operator, this mother of two adult children says that she has a second job—taking care of her mother. Mary's mother lives in her own apartment and can cook for herself, but needs help with other daily living needs, especially when her gout and arthritis flare up. When she has to work, Mary pays her sister to help make sure that her mother has what she needs for the day and gets what she needs from the store. On her days off, Mary cleans up her mother's home, handles her affairs, and takes her mother to doctor appointments. She also gives her mother daily showers because a recent bathtub fall made her mother afraid to shower independently. Mary's mother doesn't like the idea of her daughter attempting to juggle work and the responsibility of taking care of her. She knows that Mary works a lot and doesn't want to be a bother to Mary. And though Mary does not mind taking care of her mother, she acknowledges that she doesn't "have a life."

She spends the vast majority of each day balancing work and family obligations.

This juggling act is not new to tightrope walkers like Mary. She had her daughter at seventeen and her son at nineteen. If being a working teen mom wasn't enough, the dissolution of her marriage of twenty years compounded the complexities of her life. She did not expect her husband to choose drinking over his family, but since he "could not put the bottle down," in her late thirties, Mary tried to see her divorce as the start of new beginnings. In this reinvention period, Mary struggled to make ends meet as a WestCAT employee by working as a Target associate during her split shifts.

Mary did not gain access to her dream job—one that she could retire from—until she became an AC Transit employee. However, her mounting stress and the back pain that began after she started operating AC Transit equipment three years ago is beginning to affect her work performance. She worries she will not be able to keep her job; at times, she can't even lift her arms above her head due to back pain and repetitive stress injuries. Most often, she is able to juggle work and life responsibilities with ease, but some days are harder. "I just can't catch a break," she said, lamenting mounting family responsibilities and workplace expectations.

Mary's sister is unreliable and her mother's needs continue to escalate. Mary promised her mother that she wouldn't let her down, and she intends to keep her word. But, she needs to figure out how to be there to cover her mother's needs while also handling her work schedule, aches and pains, and the stress of getting written up at work for showing up late and, in some cases, failing to show up as scheduled. AC Transit's random drug testing system also gives Mary plenty of chances to lose her job; she is randomly selected to test for drug use several times a month. She mentioned that she was "quite puzzled" that she keeps getting "randomly" selected. "AC Transit has over 1,300 drivers," she said. "How is my name popping up all the time? I don't understand." Mary was not the first transit operator I spoke with who voiced that concern. Nor would she and her colleagues be the first workers suspected of using drugs to manage life and work conflicts. Historically, bus and train operator positions have been high injury, high stress jobs in which workers report persistent health problems and sometimes self-medicate or miss work as ways to cope with work fatigue, stress and injuries, and work/life conflicts.

Mary wishes she could be in two places at one time; the fact that she can't leads to feelings of inadequacy at home and work. "When it's all said and done," she told me, "everything is on me; I have to make the best out of what I have." If Mary fails to balance work and family, she understands that she will not be able to care for herself or manage her mother's care. "I'm stuck," she concluded, "because I can't win for losing."

Similar to other workers in the postindustrial era, low-skilled African American women workers like Mary have experienced profound changes in job quality and rewards over the past thirty to forty years that make it difficult to handle work and life pressures. The complexities and demands of the new service economy have produced what Arlie Russell Hochschild refers to as a "time bind." It never leaves enough time and energy to manage household and work responsibilities. In turn, both home and work lives suffer because workers with domestic responsibilities experience scheduling pressures and personal conflicts stemming from their attempts to balance incompatible demands.

Some researchers suggest that working women like Mary may find relief from work/life conflicts by reducing paid work hours during childbearing years and opting for a "scenic route" (or the "Mommy Track") as opposed to the "fast track" career model. This approach sees working mothers as disadvantaged by conventional work schedules and argues that employers could go a long way to support contemporary families by implementing part-time work arrangements.[1] However, like most previous research, Hochschild and other researchers have primarily focused on how *professional* women manage work/life conflicts. The majority of employed women, especially African American women, however, depend on low-level service jobs that *require* them to work part-time shifts and multiple jobs. Balancing work and family obligations hardly comes into this equation.

Working-class women can't afford to take the "scenic route." They *must* work, as often as possible. They are, many times, the lone providers for their families. In this book, I tell the story of how working-class African American women made inroads into a difficult and stressful, but secure, unionized occupation, only to have the quality of their positions disintegrate as the economy changed. I examine how the relationship between work and family becomes complicated by workplace norms and practices by exploring African American women's work conditions, their perceptions of these conditions, the institutional practices and policies that govern workplace relations, and the strategies women use to manage workplace pressures. In addition to the society-wide trends that have eroded their status and security, I show how their employer and their union, which *should* have been their staunch defender, contributed to discriminatory treatment and the erosion of their job status.

While I broadly examine the structure of opportunity available to transit operators in the post–Affirmative Action era, I concentrate on African American women workers, whose experiences in semiskilled jobs have been underexplored.[2] Their work experiences cannot be summed up by extending existing scholarship on African American male workers or White women workers. In fact, current scholarship suggests that their experiences in both female-dominated and male-dominated workplaces are distinctive from those of other workers.

African American women workers, who predominately worked as domestics throughout the first half of the twentieth century, initially made tremendous gains as a result of industrial restructuring.[3] They increased their visibility substantially in service sector jobs that historically hired White women, including retail trade, personal and business services, as well as professional services. By 1970, nearly four times as many African American women were working in clerical and sales work than in 1950.[4] As African American women gained ground in occupations that traditionally restricted employment to White women, most of their employment gains between 1960 and 1980 were in male-intensive services industries (like transportation, utilities, and public administration) that had undergone a great deal of restructuring due to deregulation, increased price competition, and the intensive pressure to reduce costs.[5]

Despite the improvements in their structure of opportunity, African American women workers have found that the expansion in their structure of opportunity did not lead to a "Promised Land" flowing with job security, career advancement, or persistent wage parity. By the mid-1980s, sharp cutbacks in government and service employment began to seriously dampen what progress they'd made.[6] Although African American women's level of educational attainment improved between the 1980s and 1990s, their likelihood of being poor was higher in 1989 than in 1969.[7] Moreover, between 1969 and 1983, their official unemployment rate increased from 8 to 17 percent.[8]

Younger cohorts of African American women workers have experienced gains in the labor market, but, on average, African American women workers remain distinctly disadvantaged. Recent trends indicate that African American women still primarily work nonprofessional and nontechnical low-skilled jobs, regardless of educational attainment. With declining opportunities in the public sector and the expansion of part-time employment, these workers are also less likely to find gainful employment. They are overrepresented in occupations that receive less compensation than what is earned by similarly situated White women. African American women were also distinctly disadvantaged in jobs that converted from men's work to women's work. Of these converted jobs, African American women have a history of being relegated to the worst and unhealthiest positions.[9] Transit operator positions are included among these, particularly given that job tenure within this occupation has been correlated with health problems ranging from aching backs to gastrointestinal disorders and sleep problems.[10]

My goal in this book is to understand the rise of contingent employment arrangements in a public sector service occupation, as experienced by African American women workers and to explore how those workers cope with an occupation that has transformed from a coveted occupation to a desegregated dead-end job. In telling the story of African American women transit operators at AC Transit from 1974 to 2009, I am telling a particular story of one group of marginalized workers in the United States. But I am also telling the story of many segments of the low-skilled workforce: the workplace experiences documented in this book are directly related to trends that have emerged in other occupations and industries. First, transit operators have the experience of boom and bust that many workers have endured throughout the last forty to fifty years. When African American workers initially gained access to transit operator positions, these jobs were well paid and offered mobility. With declines in public transit funding and the use of public transit, declines in compensation and working conditions as well as increased scrutiny of workers and diminished opportunities for management positions that might survive a downturn soured a once promising industry. Likewise, after World War II, various low-skilled industries, particularly the auto and steel industries, opened blue-collar opportunities for many African American and White ethnic male blue-collar workers. They came with difficult and oftentimes strenuous working conditions, but they were opportunities. Decades later, the structure of opportunity within these jobs has changed for the worse. Production lines have been cut, the use of permanent workers reduced, and the availability of work halted with the rise of neoliberalism and economic restructuring.

Second, while researchers pay a great deal of attention to neoliberal economic trends and shifts prompted by globalization in the contemporary labor market, this book documents the emergence of neoliberal *employment practices* that include the increasing use of subcontracting and contingent work arrangements. These changes are being implemented in occupations that employ a large segment of the American workforce. Meanwhile, the employment relationships that were once applied to African American men and women workers are now affecting other groups. As I argue in chapter 2, the social closure prevalent in the transit industry that primarily excluded African Americans from coveted rail and transit jobs until the early 1960s was implemented through the collaborative efforts of business owners, business organizations, unions, and the state. In the contemporary labor market, employers and business community associations continue to use the government, courts, and other entities to undermine workers, typically by lobbying the government to classify workers (like truck drivers, cab operators, and delivery drivers) as independent contractors excluded from labor protection under the National Labor Relations Act. Even one of the fastest growing jobs, home health care work, is exempt from this legislation. State support for business initiatives to reclassify workers to subcontractor status (including stock clerks employed by large stores and grocery chains as well as waitresses and bar maids) helps employers avoid wage and hour regulations that have long protected workers. Walmart's subcontracted stock workers recently secured a $21 million dollar settlement with Schneider Logistics Inc., one of Walmart's largest distribution subcontractors, for alleged wage theft. The workers, who load and unload shipping containers into trailers for Walmart, claimed that they were illegally paid by a piece rate and fired when they complained about their wages. These workers also alleged that they earned less than minimum wage for working double shifts and did not have access to required breaks during a seven-day work week. Work is harder to find than ever, and the jobs that are available are becoming worse, not better.

In addition, hiring patterns and shifts in the structure of opportunity within AC Transit provide an early example of the shift from full-time to part-time and split-shift work arrangements. The numbers of African American women employed by AC Transit in 1974 and 1975 climbed despite the fact that AC Transit was beginning a period of declining employment and budgets due, in part, to the beginning of BART (Bay Area Rapid Transit) operations in 1974 and funding decisions at the regional level that favored BART. Although AC Transit eventually found ways to secure funds by agreeing to assist BART and to extend their services in East Oakland, Emeryville, Richmond, El Cerrito, and Albany (areas that were underserved by BART), AC Transit contended with budget issues as it eliminated routes serving dense and decentralized communities. In this context, African American women operators, as shown in chapter 3, were placed in less favorable divisions within AC Transit. These offered less recovery time as well as limited earnings and promotion opportunities. Over time, though AC Transit continued to hire African American women, most of these workers were secured to work on a part-time basis or to work a split shift for less money and fewer benefits.

Contingent workplace arrangements have become more popular across industries. Between the 1980s and 1990s, the number of temporary and contingent workers in the labor force tripled. Arne Kalleberg notes that this employment arrangement became prominent in the 1970s in response to the emergence of labor laws crafted to protect permanent employees and to global economic changes that increased competition. Converting to a contingent labor force has done more than weaken the bargaining power of labor and threatens job security. This switch to a more "flexible" workforce also allows employers to sidestep payroll taxes and unemployment insurance, passing rising health and pension costs on to contingent, low-skilled workers.[11]

Lastly, these days, it is not uncommon to hear stories about "lazy" and "mean" transit operators dropping riders off blocks before their stops and leaving earlier than scheduled. Transit operators share with other workers a perception that they are entitled, lazy, and/or incompetent and thus do not deserve even their wages and benefits. These public narratives of cultural deficit and dependency are not specific to the transit operator experience, and such tropes are increasingly used by employers, lobbyists, and politicians to delegitimize workers' claims to better compensation and employment benefits. Across the nation, public service workers, including teachers and nurses, have been characterized as overpaid "babysitters" whose wages and benefits are driving up public education and health care costs. Republican Governor Scott Walker effectively used this narrative in Wisconsin to undermine public sector unions, and he has been motivated to further discourage the labor protections secured by professors employed by state colleges and universities. In Governor Walker's current campaign, he has stated that he aims to eliminate teacher tenure, create gateway plans to allow people with "real-life experience" to be licensed to teach in public schools, and include state bureaucrats in hiring and promotion decisions and efforts to develop college curricula.

Meanwhile, many Americans were shocked when *Mother Jones* magazine posted a video of a private political fundraiser in Florida where 2012 Republican Presidential candidate Mitt Romney proclaimed that most of President Barack Obama's support in the election would come from those "dependent" on government. He characterized these Obama supporters as the "47%" who "believe that they are victims . . . who believe that they are entitled to health care, to food, to housing. . . . You name it." These people, Romney claimed, refuse to take "personal responsibility and care for their lives." Romney's statement seemed to dismiss close to a majority of Americans as undeserving of political attention—not "givers" and "makers," but "takers," a class of dependents who lack the values, ability, and persistence to assume responsibility or to succeed on their individual merits. But this assault on the middle and working class may have been less shocking to those who know the long history of political ideas in which the poor and marginalized have been depicted not as fellow citizens, but as lazy bottom feeders, unworthy of political voice and sidelined by their own depraved cultural values and personal failures.[12]

Romney's dismissal implicitly invoked long-standing political ideologies and cultural norms that have depicted social welfare policies as creating (and reproducing) a population of people dependent on government and lacking in individual agency. These ideologies look at contemporary inequality through social lenses blind to socioeconomic structures and to the persistence of racialized and gendered power. They see affirmative action and other efforts to end institutional discrimination as undermining individual responsibility and furthering government dependency. What Romney articulated was merely an expansion of these perspectives to include, polarize, and mobilize a majority of already privileged Americans.

Though Romney tried to distance himself from his divisive comments, especially as they proved effective fodder for his Democratic opponents, his narrative echoed a long-standing tendency to conflate welfare and dependence, mobility and individual ability. Holding significant resonance in contemporary political discourse, this story suggests that access to opportunity is evenly distributed and that immobility or employment insecurity is a consequence of individual (or group) values, ambition, and ability. It suggests that we live in an equal opportunity era, in which civil rights legislation and affirmative action policies have dismantled obstacles to racial and gender equality and produced an equal playing field that no longer *needs* such policies and protections. From this perspective, persistent racial and gender inequality can be explained (and dismissed) as a consequence of cultural practices and differential values. In this study, I provide an empirically grounded critique of narratives that present inequality and employment insecurity as a consequence of individual characteristics and dismiss governmental intervention into the economy and labor market as outdated and dangerous, promoting a culture of dependency and entitlements.[13] I interrogate such narratives by focusing on the work experiences of those who have been depicted as the "most dependent": African American women.

Hard Work Is Not Enough is an extended case study of African American women transit operators that explores the historical context in which they entered transit work and the processes and factors that have limited their career mobility. What can such a case study contribute to our understanding of the broader structures of mobility and the narrative of government dependency? Rather than a broad swipe at Romney's 47 percent, this careful and comprehensive case study of those who have been most consistently depicted as government dependents will help us understand the persistent obstacles faced by working-class African American women in the labor market. It will also help disentangle and highlight the social antagonisms, economic hurdles, and institutional practices that limit the opportunities of low-skilled workers more generally. Finally, it will make clearer the limitations of narratives about values and governmental dependency as determinative of social position and career mobility.

The empirical work in this book documents that as African Americans entered this workplace in significant numbers as a consequence of civil rights gains, the union and the employer both adopted a range of strategies to constrict the opportunities available to these newly hired workers. It assesses three decades (1974–2009) of shifts in the work culture and discipline practices within transit workplaces that have eroded the quality of the work environment for all workers, but hit

African American women workers especially hard. In gathering evidence of disparate employer policing, I argue that AC Transit played a role in reconstituting the social hierarchy by undermining the minority worker's job security.

Work progress and job security are influenced by the economic, social, and institutional features of the workplace. African American women were more likely to enter AC Transit under neoliberal employment arrangements as part-time workers hired to work during early morning and evening shifts, when it was especially difficult to secure child care. As workers who were not union members, part-time transit operators employed by AC Transit had few established rights and limited access to fringe benefits associated with the transit operator position. Many part-time operators, by 1989, had been working for AC Transit for several years and did not have access to important fringe benefits. While earning relatively good wages with AC Transit, they did not have vacation time, sick leave, and health insurance.

Accordingly, the findings in this book demonstrate the extent to which workplace punishment functions to maintain the status quo within workplaces. Not only was AC Transit quick to discipline workers, it is clear from arbitrations and discipline reports that the heavily African American and women districts were disciplined much more harshly than the transit district that housed the majority of White male transit operators. As such, many of the bureaucratic policies designed to increase worker productivity were actually used to reconstitute inequality and preserve status hierarchy. Although AC Transit eventually altered its hiring process to the point of significantly decreasing the number of White and male new hires, workplace progress is limited by AC Transit's disproportionate implementation of arbitrary rules designed to manage worker conduct through harsh penalties.

Lastly, in this study, I document how a two-tiered system emerged within AC Transit. It extends privileges and protections to some workers, while rendering others vulnerable to internal and external threats to their job. African American women transit operators I studied had a tough time maintaining their employment because of the labor union's seniority system as well as AC Transit's placement decisions, which had them working the worst shifts in the toughest neighborhoods serviced by the company. AC Transit also encouraged the development of a two-tiered labor structure by protecting privileged workers with seniority from harsh discipline, while treating new employees like seasonal workers who could be easily dismissed. AC Transit reinforced its differential treatment of new African American women hires by making placement decisions that impaired the mobility of workers. With the two-tiered system in place, low-tier workers faced a slew of problems that ranged from demands to work longer hours to the deterioration of work resources, intensified work rules and misconduct penalties, hazardous working conditions, and diminished autonomy on the job. Especially between 1975 and 1985, the union, Amalgamated Transit Union (ATU) 192, declined to fiercely advocate for new workers. Instead, the union devoted its efforts to preserving seniority rights, tabling many of the concerns brought by African American women workers, including the need for recovery time (break periods) and ways to address problems with securing child care. I document how workers' declining control over the bureaucratic policies and conditions of their work has contributed to the downward shifts in their structure of opportunity.

Organization

This book chronicles the subtleties and consequences of institutionalized workplace discrimination within the context of an urban transit workplace in the San Francisco Bay Area. It captures how the tradeoffs between productivity and equality have made and adapted after previously excluded workers were integrated into this workplace. By exploring low-skilled work from the perspective of the workers, I observe how less desired workers are treated when they gain access to a desegregating but declining occupation. Their stories illustrate the institutional and structural features that shape workplace realities and the hurdles they must navigate. In particular, I chronicle workers' struggles as mothers in a workplace that is not "mommy friendly" and hasn't gotten around to adjusting work norms to accommodate working mothers. The stories explore what drives a worker's desire to quit even when she depends on the job to provide for her family. They document why some workers can't hold onto these jobs, despite their best intentions.

Chapter 2 situates this analysis by documenting the history of African American and female employment in the urban transit industry from the mid-1940s to the early 1970s, with particular interest on labor relations within Key System Transit Lines, the predecessor of AC Transit District. Drawing from allegations of discrimination filed with the Fair Employment Practice Committee and the National War and Labor

Board, in addition to lawsuits filed against AC Transit in the 1970s, this chapter captures how demographic shifts in the East Bay area shaped the stance and strategies of employers and unions opposed to employing women and racial minorities as transit operators, closing the opportunities available to African American women in particular within a context of shifting social, economic, and bureaucratic forces in the post–Affirmative Action era.

Chapter 3 describes relevant shifts in the working conditions within AC Transit and captures the overt and covert discrimination African American women faced when they first entered this workplace as transit operators. While primarily documenting the rise of bureaucratic policies and their influence on the work conditions *after* African American women began working for AC Transit as transit operators in large numbers, this chapter also reports on the scope of African American women's reception in this workplace by documenting their experiences working in other capacities within the company. Still, chapter 3 is primarily concerned with changes in the nature of transit operator work and the degree to which firm and labor union opposition to desegregating coveted positions limited the structure of opportunity available to women and racial/ethnic minority workers. This chapter documents how African American women transit operators were positioned within the company, as well as the options and restrictions they encountered. Respondents featured in this chapter point out how their racialization and sexualization on the job was reinforced by workplace norms that shaped patterns of interaction and mobility. Their resistance to efforts to limit their advancement within this social space is witnessed through their individual and collective efforts to prove their competence on the job.

While considering the perspectives of AC Transit and ATU 192, chapters 4 and 5 document the rise of worker-centered reforms and how they dramatically altered the quality of the job and intensified work/life conflicts. Factoring in AC Transit's rationalizations for downward shifts in job quality and the constraints that undermined ATU 192's capacity to adequately address these shifts, chapter 4 documents increasing pressure to perform despite workplace hazards and work/life imbalances that made keeping the job an uphill battle for African American women workers. With correspondence between management and union leaders from labor archives, litigation against the firm, interviews with African American women employed as transit operators and transit supervisors, and grievance and arbitration data, I illustrate the demise of the old world of transit operating that offered good wages, benefits, and predictability on the job. Evidence suggests that transit operating became increasingly stressful throughout the period of study due to the implementation of institutional strategies. African American women transit operators report good wages, but a host of barriers to their occupational advancement, all affected by perceptions of their work commitment, declining job conditions, and intense pressure to perform in the workplace as resources are slashed.

Chapter 5 captures the consequences of worker-centered reforms used to discipline "unproductive" work habits as well as the rise of drug testing in the urban transit industry. These developments have shaped the workplace experiences of all AC Transit operators. This chapter highlights respondents' perpetual problems with close supervision, coworker hostility, and differential treatment as both women and African Americans. Evidence from the Federal Transit Administration further illustrates serious problems with this specific employer's implementation of its random drug-testing program and its consistent citing for inability to comply with federal standards and equally apply drug testing throughout the workplace.

Chapter 6 presents an overview of how industrial declines, persistent social tensions, and institutional shifts in the labor process have influenced the structure of occupational opportunities available to African American women workers throughout the period of study. Since it has been established that screening practices and human resource policies have become increasingly important to understanding opportunity shifts and workplace inequality, we need a framework that helps make sense of how these forms of social control in the labor process not only affect who gets hired, but also who *advances*. In chapter 6, I advance such a framework. I take into account the structural changes within a workplace that include diminished labor power and truncated career ladders, and I reflect on the function of shifts in labor process and how they affect workers' reception and evaluation in these settings.

I dive into the world of African American women transit operators employed by AC Transit to show the specific ways in which the employer and union contributed to the maintenance of status segregation and inequality in one representative post–Affirmative Action era workplace. This extended case study is a microcosm of neoliberal employment relations that features the social, economic, and bureaucratic constraints that African American women in desegregating workplaces confront, as well as how the consequences of these hurdles manifest in their lives. Transit districts are federal contractors required to hire a diverse workforce, despite their history of strong opposition to external efforts to diversify coveted positions. Since there is a great deal to learn from the actions of resistant firms and unions forced to balance their preconceptions of excluded low-skilled workers with business necessities, the terms and conditions of AC Transit's employment of African American women transit operators are the chief concerns of this book.

1

Concepts and Methods

Understanding Opportunity Shifts among Transit Operators in the Post–Affirmative Action Era

In this study, I sought out answers to the following questions: To what extent is African American women transit operators' employment progress shaped by workplace conditions? How do workplace policies, tensions, and divisions influence their structure of opportunity? How is workplace progress related to work/life imbalances? And to what degree has union advocacy improved workplace conditions and attempts to address personal concerns including work/life imbalances and physical injury on the job? In this chapter, I describe the concepts and discussions that shaped my responses and present the data and methods that informed my analysis of workplace progress among African American women transit operators.

Three distinctive perspectives dominate discussions of low-skilled women's progress in the workplace. Scholars tend to focus on neoliberal changes in employment relations, persistent race and gender bias and discrimination, and the diminishing role of labor unions in protecting workers and helping them to advance and gain stability in the workplace.

Neoliberal Changes in Employment Relations among Low-Skilled Workforce

Low-skilled American workers have fallen on hard times, generally thought to stem from economic restructuring and shifts from goods-producing to service and information-producing economies characterized by lower wages.[1] By 1986, service industries made up 75 percent of all nonfarm wage and salary employment and 53 percent of real domestic output, while employment in manufacturing declined significantly. Just over 27 percent of full-time workers were employed by firms in manufacturing in 1970, declining to 15 percent by 2000.[2] This structural shift was brought on by technological innovations, the exportation of low-skilled jobs to low-wage countries, and the globalization of markets that have increased the demand for the production of high-quality but low-cost goods. Those companies and types of work that remain in the United States require ever more skilled workers, increasing inequality between highly educated workers and their counterparts with less education and fewer marketable skills. Since it is harder to find a good paying job, many low-skilled workers struggle to manage familial obligations. They are underemployed or trapped in jobs that cannot provide the income, stability, and opportunity they need.

Workers have seen declines in their workplace outcomes because employers have gone to great lengths throughout the neoliberal era to cut labor costs whenever possible. Part of the business community's cost-cutting strategy has involved uniting to defeat labor law reform and taxation, while working to roll back government regulations of workplace safety and health.[3] As a result, in sectors that are predominate employers of women of color (like retail), the structure of opportunity has changed for the worse. Brown et al. note that, over the past twenty years, a job in the retail industry, especially in a supermarket, has shifted from a "full-time, relatively well-paid position (often unionized) to a job with irregular and part time hours, low pay, and few chances for mobility."[4] Similarly, in the face of intensifying global competition, employers like those within the hospitality industry have opted to "do more with less," a strategy that cuts costs by way of wage freezes and reduced work hours. As a result, the problems that workers like room cleaners in hotels endure include unpredictable schedules and being pressured to meet impossible room quotas, as well as contending with on-the-job injuries and insufficient breaks throughout the work day.[5] In conjunction with the increasing use of on-call workers, the average hours of room cleaning per worker have reduced from forty hours a week in 1960 to thirty-one hours a week in 2000.[6]

When it comes to outsourcing and other cost-cutting measures, the hospitality industry is not alone, and the changes make earning a family-sustaining wage and developing a career nearly impossible. Hospitals, for instance, have redefined job positions as a way to cut costs. Many routine tasks previously assigned to registered nurses (including taking vital signs and drawing blood), have shifted to nursing assistants, allowing companies to cut the hours and duties of the more highly paid registered nurses. Hospitals are also more frequently outsourcing management, instead of hiring supervisors from their current workforce or through direct employment. Job placement companies like Sodexho and Service Master supply managers to supervise workers in food services and housekeeping within hospitals, cutting off a once-promising career ladder of internal promotion.[7]

Maintenance of Status Segregation within the Workplace

While occupational returns are shaped by the skills that workers bring to the labor market, just as important is how workers are perceived and where they are positioned within any particular workplace. Occupations are social fields, containing systems of domination that often reflect or exploit antagonisms within local areas or the broader society.[8] Employers play key roles in setting the ground rules that affect workers' everyday lives and in instituting practices and rankings that reproduce or modify existing social hierarchies.

Structural studies exploring how racial and gender inequality operates at the occupation level generally explore how organizational and administrative actions produce and reconstitute racial and gender inequality. Most structural theorists draw heavily on social closure and the visibility discrimination theory in their investigations of how job contexts and deskilling restrict access to authority and job autonomy.[9] Drawing on Blalock's "visibility-discrimination" hypothesis, structural theorists maintain that occupation racial inequality is more intense when African Americans make up a significant percentage of the workforce.[10] Most of the attention within this line of inquiry focuses on how African American–dominated jobs exploit workers by paying African American workers less than similarly situated White workers, limiting mobility and excluding racial minorities from positions of authority.[11]

Sociologists also argue that workers are disadvantaged in the labor market due to the statistical discrimination (i.e., negative stereotyping) they encounter at work.[12] For instance, regardless of their actual parenting status, African American women workers are perceived as single mothers, and, in turn, are viewed as unprepared and weakly committed to paid labor due to family responsibilities.[13] Furthermore, structural scholars examining the discriminatory effects of work and family workplace policies warn against restructuring work schedules to contend with work and family imbalances because schedules have been found to further intensify the gender division of labor within workplaces and hinder women's rise to upper management. To this end, some structural innovations, like flexible work schedules and mentoring programs, have been helpful to women workers. Other workplace management actions have negatively affected women's ability to advance.[14]

Unions

Since collective bargaining agreements typically clarify job classifications and wage scales and specify promotion and dismissal guidelines, unionization is considered a means to protect workers against arbitrary, firm-level actions. Unionism provides a social and economic good to workers as organized labor works to protect internal career ladders and promote pay equality within job classifications. Unionization also improves workplace equality by helping to create and enforce bureaucratic rules that weaken management's ability to discriminate and discharge workers at will.[15]

By specifying the conditions under which employees are promoted and fired, unions act as labor market agents that make efforts to secure good working conditions and fair pay for workers. Due to their efforts, union workers are more likely to have guaranteed pensions and job-related health coverage than nonunion workers. Union workers also earn, on average, more than nonunion workers and benefit from the union's collective bargaining power to negotiate with employers.

Despite the potential benefits of being a union member, however, in the post–World War II era unionization rates began to decline. Declines in unionization have been attributed to the geographic redistribution of the business community to nonunion areas, but the decline in union membership was also spearheaded by employer resistance to unionization and postindustrial shifts from a manufacturing economy to a service-based economy.[16] Scholars contend that downward shifts in unionization matter much more than industrial and occupational shifts, because changes in unionization can account for 10 percent of the wage gaps observed among young Black and White women workers between 1973 and 1991.[17]

In this study, I build on those perspectives while emphasizing that these explanations, collectively and individually, cannot account for the contemporary shifts in the nature of low-skilled work. Nor can these perspectives account for the causes and consequences of work and family conflicts among low-skilled workers. Most importantly, it is rarely acknowledged that dead-end jobs, often called "contingent" or "precarious," are not evenly distributed among all sectors of the population.

Indeed, African American women are especially likely to hold these jobs (and to *not* hold other, more secure jobs). Furthermore, we have learned a great deal from quantitative analyses of substantiated discrimination claims and equal employment opportunity (EEO) data,[18] but these descriptions of race and sexual harassment cannot examine the microaggressions and other subtle forms of institutional discrimination at play within workplaces. Since the vast majority of extant studies has employed an ahistorical view of firm-level policies or focused explicitly on individual experiences with biased managers, it is unclear how industry-level mechanisms translate into racial and gender stratification in the workplace, especially with regard to career mobility on the job.[19]

Similarly, we know that unions have not always been open to or helpful for all workers. Unions are social institutions subject to ideological assumptions and constraints, especially those pertaining to race and gender. From the introduction of "separate but equal" union locals to the advocacy of anti-immigrant policy, U.S. labor history is full of examples that detail exclusionary efforts made to keep workers of color out of unions. Exclusionary practices have included restricting admissions to apprenticeship programs, denying journeymen cards to African American nonunionists, refusing union admission, and creating segregated auxiliary locals for African Americans and other racial/ethnic minority workers. Unions have also worked to reinforce White male privilege by maintaining seniority systems that limit the progress of new hires.[20]

Since the passage of antidiscrimination laws, the treatment of workers of color within the labor movement has improved substantially. Although African American workers in particular continue to be treated as "destabilizing element[s] that needed to be controlled," they are no longer barred from these organizations and have, in some cases, gained access to leadership positions (even though in many cases these positions have been stripped of power). The fact remains that the legacy of union resistance against the integration of African American workers who became "an irritant in the ointment for organized labor" lives on due to the inability of many unions and unionists to understand the politics of race and how the relative privilege of White workers weakens prospects for true worker solidarity. Racial bias weakens unions. Thus, this legacy not only limits the opportunity for working-class mobilization, but also, as Fletcher argues, "challenges the authenticity of organized labor's commitment, not only to organize the unorganized, but to the belief that an injury to one is truly an injury to all."[21]

Women's exclusion from labor unions and positions of power within the labor movement played a critical role in shaping women workers' labor circumstances. Even when women worked alongside male workers, they were not asked to participate in organizing campaigns and were excluded from union leadership, actions which marginalized women's concerns and reinforced their status in the workplace. While labor market opportunities created for women by World War II and the feminist movement in the 1960s and 1970s altered the union's policies, conflict still exists along gender lines. Gendered conflict is most evident in sexual harassment cases in the workplace, in which female and male members' interests are in direct opposition.[22] Despite the fact that the U.S. Supreme Court recognized sexual harassment as a form of sex discrimination under Title VII in 1986, union women who complain to stewards about sexual harassment often encounter resistance and hostility. Many are also left to figure out how to tolerate a hostile work environment, because they are thought to have voluntarily "assum[ed] the risk of harassment" by joining a male-dominated workforce.[23]

Due to the limits of studies that are overtly structural or dependent on self-reported data, in addition to the limitations associated with assuming that unionization can address the concerns of *all* workers, this study relies on a variety of data over a forty year period. This enables me to develop a grounded account of the modern labor movement and its capacity to advocate for marginalized, low-skilled workers. I examine the impact of the social, economic, and bureaucratic sources on workplace inequality within one mass transit workplace because establishment-level research lets us see the extent to which workers' experiences are affected by the structural characteristics of the work environment *and* by microlevel mechanisms that undermine EEO goals within the workplace. This case study of transit operators' work in the San Francisco Bay Area provides an opportunity to delve into the underlying mechanisms driving the patterns observed in the statistical analyses, especially as they relate to the downward shifts in the structure of work available to low-skilled workers.[24] While I assume a priori relationships between the bureaucratic developments and workplace culture, this case is exploratory and designed to contribute to theoretical discussions about shifts in the nature of low-skilled work and its effect on marginalized women workers.

Since various factors contribute to the hurdles that workers encounter in the workplace, the theory of intersectionality is especially useful in this analysis.[25] We limit ourselves when we attempt to examine African American women's plight in the workforce with the analytical tools calibrated to explore the unique experiences that African American men face, because we miss the salience of paternalism that gender bias encourages and that class bias motivates. Likewise, if the mechanisms shaping African American women's workplace experiences are reduced to sex-typing and gender bias, we overlook how their structure of opportunity is shaped by race-based antagonisms motivated by group competition and perceptions of social honor that mitigate their claim to social, economic, and political resources and justify the terms and conditions of social closure. Therefore, I argue that modern race and gender bias, as a complex and inextricable bind for African American women in the workplace, manifests as social tensions and neutral institutional efforts that function to contest and challenge new hires' access to progress by undermining their ability to keep the job. This way of examining intersectional institutional discrimination (or race *and* gender bias) is a departure. Furthermore, while individual-level feelings of hostility and intolerance can help account for stalls in workplace progress, reliance on individual feelings alone cannot capture how group position is maintained in the workplace. By examining how group position is preserved through contestation, scholars are better positioned to explore how status group power is conceived and how preexisting power relations are maintained. As a mechanism that functions to maintain the position of the dominant group, race and gender prejudice has the capacity to shape workplace norms and policies that determine a group's relative status.

Recent research supports the need for more situated examinations of EEO progress within establishments and demonstrates the extent to which within-firm processes are racialized and gendered. In their study of four medical firms, Gerstel and Clawson found that employer practices and policies for nursing assistants employed by two different nursing homes differed substantially with regard to requests for time off. The nursing home in which 88 percent of the aides were people of color, tended to rely on draconian policies and enforcement procedures that restricted the nursing aides' ability to request time off and subjected them to harsh punishment if these policies were violated. Meanwhile, the nursing home that hired fewer people of color as aides (25 percent of workplace) implemented similar policies, but was more willing to accommodate individual requests for flexibility and time off.[26] Drawing from establishment-level studies like Gerstel and Clawson's, this study is

designed to develop a grounded interpretation of the role that bureaucratic policies, economic constraints, and social tensions that stem from
hiring African American women have played in shaping their progress
as transit operators between 1974 and 2005.[27] The values and the practices of the transit employer as well, as the labor union featured in this
study, are important to understanding manifestations of workplace
inequality. The social aspects of this research are captured through interactions with workers; correspondence among workers, the union, and
management; lawsuits filed by workers and the union; and newspaper
stories and trade journal coverage documenting the nature of employment
relations within the firm. Economic sources refer to shifts in promotional
opportunities for workers and the material well-being of the employer,
workers, and the industry.

In my effort to capture the bureaucratic sources of employment (in)
security, I acknowledge the role that neutral business practices play in
limiting workers' access to jobs. I use disparate impact theory to understand the consequences of new worker policies and procedures that
emerged in AC Transit just as it began to desegregate transit operator
positions in the mid-1970s. Institutional practices and social interactions may be deemed discriminatory when there is evidence of system-
atic patterns of promoting unequal treatment of racial/ethnic minorities
as a group. Given the evidence regarding how ostensibly neutral employment practices adversely impacted low-skilled workers of color,[28] it is also
plausible that *after* workers are hired, employers create further "neutral" policies and procedures that result in privileging some groups over
others.

The goal in a disparate impact analysis is to examine the extent to
which neutral firm policies have adversely affected a protected class. In
order to employ a disparate impact analysis, I examine the extent to which
employment practices, policies, and relations disproportionately impact
the work careers of newly hired workers. I do so by documenting the
neoliberal changes in employment relations and work policies used to
curb absences, as well as examining discipline records to determine the
degree to which these bureaucratic practices and policies impose a significant adverse impact on newly hired African American women workers
(and not others).[29] By legitimizing unrestrained capitalism, neoliberalism,
an ideology that has shaped how employers govern workers since the
market crisis of the 1970s,[30] has provided the business community the
opportunity to institutionalize modern forms of control through

policies that contest and challenge redistributive goals. Aimed at maximizing profits and the distribution of goods, neoliberal governance has empowered the business community to take a more substantial role in regulating social life by legitimizing a whole set of practices to surveil, discipline, and punish workers, while continuing to benefit from their labor. The business community relies on cultural and political mechanisms, which Bourdieu refers to as "techniques of manipulation"[31] to blind the public to the consequences of their market-driven ideology.[32]

Under the neoliberal regime, a culture of omnipresent surveillance has ignited privacy concerns; the new forms of power are more pervasive than the presence of an overseer, an inquisitive boss, or a micromanaging shift supervisor.[33] As chapter 5 will show, drug testing and worker monitoring represent substantial departures from traditional forms of workplace control. The main difference in modern controls, as Gilliom puts it, "is that government and corporate authorities no longer need to discover misbehavior through verbal testimony or chance observation because they can cut through the human faculties of secrecy, deception, or denial, look inside the body, and see what the individual has been doing."[34]

Bureaucratic sources of employment insecurity are also examined by documenting institutional efforts and rationales for contesting the rights of workers through the implementation of managerial policies that increase the risk of personal injury. Differential exposure to injury on the job is a significant indicator to consider in attempts to understand employment insecurity and inequality in the United States. Despite the passage of the Occupational Safety and Health Act of 1970, many American workers still encounter workplace health challenges that range from anxiety and stress to poisoning, nonfatal injuries, and musculoskeletal disorders. Workers of color are disproportionately situated in hazardous jobs. Blue collar and manual jobs that neglect to adapt to individuals' physical capabilities also seriously affect the health and career mobility of women workers.[35]

The Importance of Studying Transit Operating

I focus on the experiences of African American women transit operators employed by AC Transit because their experiences provide an instructive illustration of within-firm processes and the labor union's reactions to external pressures to desegregate male-dominated, low-skilled workplaces. Private transit companies have an extensive history of avoiding African American workers and limiting them to menial jobs, and transit unions have been equally committed to preserving White male privilege. This has encouraged social divisions and created a great divide between workers and their leadership. Transportation labor associations like the ATU and the Transport Workers Union (TWU) emerged at the beginning of the twentieth century as representatives of less than two hundred streetcar workers per firm. The number of workers supported by transit unions did not begin to expand until the rising cost of gas, an increased need for public transportation in urban areas, and the financial collapse of privately owned transportation firms led to the passage of federal and state laws designed to support publicly owned mass transit agencies by the mid-1960s.[36]

The transit workplace thus became, necessarily, more diverse, while the leadership with most unions continued to consist of White men loyal to high-seniority workers (also predominately White men). The most significant hurdle to creating an inclusive labor movement within the transit industry has been unionists' inability, as Gould put it, to determine "how to reconcile equal employment opportunity today with seniority expectations based on yesterday's built-in discrimination."[37] Unions like the ATU have a long history of filing motions to intervene in employment discrimination cases for the purpose of protecting the seniority rights of members who may be adversely affected by relief sought by plaintiffs that could impact shifts, vacation days, and layoffs.[38] Similarly, unions that have not directly involved themselves in litigation oftentimes resist and evade the issue of job discrimination by ignoring grievances and complaints from African American workers.[39]

The shift from a homogeneous to a diverse workforce had a profound impact on how craft associations like transportation unions engaged their members. While the TWU has a more extensive history as a democratic organization that embraces the needs of all workers, ATU was delayed in making efforts to socially integrate its membership, despite how its inaction alienated workers and limited worker mobility. Amalgamated locals restricted membership to Whites and tended to allow members more autonomy than TWU locals when dealing with racial issues. Given the union's inability to integrate the new hires, tight bonds between high seniority workers and union leadership became apparent and incredibly divisive. Due to a history of restricting African American workers' access to transit jobs, transportation unions like ATU 192 in Oakland, California, did *not* serve as vehicles for improving race and gender relations in the workplace as African American women gained access to it. The union was not prepared to take on workplace concerns that uniquely impacted women. They were set up to protect workers from economic exploitation, but were loyal to workers with the most seniority and those were, primarily, White males.[40]

Furthermore, though transit employers who relied on federal funds were expected to comply with federal and state antidiscrimination laws, many had to be *forced* to employ a diverse workforce. The urban transit industry has excluded African American workers in particular from key positions since before the 1940s.[41] While African American men were hired to work menial and dirty jobs, they were excluded from serving as conductors or engineers on the railroads, kept from working as airline pilots, and excluded from motor car positions within developing urban areas. Despite the fact that the skill requirements were low, the operation of equipment in the urban transit industry, especially in the South, was considered "White" work. Accordingly, transit employers made attempts to recruit White women as transit operators and conductors during labor shortages and periods where Black male labor was restricted to menial positions,[42] but transit employers were especially opposed to hiring racial minority women due to their assumption that these workers would be unreliable due to the likelihood of getting pregnant and not being fit to perform the work.[43] Oftentimes, within this workplace that valued "manliness," racial minority women were seen by both management and union leaders as "those people," "welfare recipients" who were "taking jobs away from men" who needed the jobs.[44]

In order to make sense of the working conditions many African American women faced as new hires in nontraditional workplaces, I focus on the working conditions of transit operators. After the 1970s, this occupation, as table 1.1 demonstrates, hired large numbers of African American women and continues to be one of the top ten employers of African American women workers. I will show how this opening arena of employment opportunity for African American women in the 1970s contracted over twenty years, becoming, instead, a place of diminished opportunity. The AC Transit story helps to demonstrate how gains from civil rights law and affirmative action could quickly change, shifting

Table 1.1 Rank of top jobs and mean incomes of high school–educated Black women by year, 1970 and 2000

	Rank of Job in 1970	Rank of Job in 2000	Rank of Mean Income in 2000	Percentage Part-Time	Percentage Covered by Union Contract
Administrative support	1	1	5	21	14.1
Sales	6	2	2	29	5
Machine operators	2	3	1	22.9	7
Hospital attendants	5	4	7	19	15.4
Cooks	*	5	4	40	4.9
Food service workers	4	6	8	61	6.9
Building service workers	*	7	9	22	19.6
Transport operators	*	8	3	46	34.8
Laborers	*	9	6	26	19.4
Personal service work	10	10	10	28	6.5
Household work	3				
Teachers	7				
Practical nursing	8				
Health technicians	9				

* Not ranked within top ten occupations.
Source: Author's calculations of Integrated Public Use Microdata Series data; ages 20–64.
Source of percentage part-time and percentage covered by union contract: Barry T. Hirsch and David A. MacPherson, *Union Membership and Earnings Data Book: Compilations from the [BLS] Current Population Survey* (Washington, D.C.: Bureau of National Affairs, 1998).

industries from labor settings of declining opportunity and declining employment due to persistent employer and union practices of exclusion and unequal treatment.

There are two types of transit operators: urban and intercity transit operators and school transit operators. School transit operators transport children to and from school and school-related events, while urban transit and intercity transit operators take people along routes within regions of a state or within a metropolitan area. Urban transit and intercity transit operators earn more than school transit operators. Just about 654,300 Americans held transit operator positions in 2012, and 74 percent of these workers were employed by schools or special client firms. By May of that year, the median annual wage for transit and intercity transit operators was $36,600, while the median annual wage for school transit operators was $28,080.

All transit operators must have a high school diploma (or its equivalent) and possess a commercial driver's license that demonstrates their ability to operate a bus and their knowledge of state and federal regulations. Local transit and intercity transit operators are responsible for collecting fares, addressing questions about routes and schedules, and announcing stops. Oftentimes transit operators are also expected to assist passengers with baggage and check the gas, oil, and water before departure if their district does not have a maintenance crew. Most are scheduled for a five-day work week (or more) and are generally well paid. According to the Occupational Outlook in 2014, AC Transit is among the highest paying transit employers in the nation at $25.14 an hour. However, to put this wage in context, the National Low Income Housing Coalition reported in 2014 that workers needed to earn $30.35 to afford a two-bedroom apartment in the East Bay area.[45]

While just over 6 percent of all American workers in 2010 were employed in transportation and material-moving occupations,[46] urban mass transit firms have significantly increased their share of women and non-White workers since the 1970s.[47] The proportion of African Americans employed by transit firms increased substantially from 3 percent in 1940 to 6 percent in 1950, 11 percent in 1960, and 25 percent in 2010.[48] The proportion of women employed by transit firms has also grown steadily from 3.1 percent of transit workers in 1940 to 43.5 percent in 2010.[49]

Increased opportunities for White men in other well-paying jobs led, by the mid-1970s, to significant advances in racialized minorities and women workers in the transit industry. Firms still avoided hiring African American women as transit operators for years, even after beginning to hire White women in the 1940s and African American men in the 1950s.

Throughout the 1970s, transit districts began hiring more African Americans, table 1.2, which illustrates the percentage of African Americans hired by AC Transit by classification between 1973 and 1976, shows that the percentage of African Americans employed in management positions increased quickly, from 7 percent to just under 12 percent in 1976. Moreover, despite a reduction in employment between 1975 and 1976, African Americans saw their total share of jobs within transit districts like AC Transit increased slightly from 30 percent in 1975 to just over 32 percent in 1976.

Table 1.2 Percentage of Blacks in AC Transit by classification and year, 1973–1976

	Year			
	1973	*1974*	*1975*	*1976*
Total employed	1,661	1,765	2,115	1,890
Total percentage of Blacks employed	24.3	27.7	30.2	32.3
Percentage of Blacks employed in service/ maintenance positions	11.7	10.6	11.8	11.8
Percentage of Blacks employed in clerical positions	5.7	8	10.9	14.3
Percentage of Blacks employed as transit operators	29.2	32	36.1	39.2
Percentage of Blacks employed in management positions	7.3	8.4	11.8	11.6

Source: Pate et al., Intervenors v. Alameda Contra Costa Transit District, September 28, 1979, 11, 16, 34.

Between 1980 and 2010, shifts in the gender composition of transit operator positions within Alameda, as illustrated in table 1.3, have been more substantial than demographic shifts observed within the state of California. There was a light *decrease* in men's share of transit operator positions, from 62 percent of transit operators in 1980 to 59 percent throughout the 2006–2010 period. Meanwhile, women workers' share of transit positions in Alameda County exploded, rising from 26 percent in 1980 to 52 percent throughout the 2006–2010 period.

Demographic shifts are much more pronounced once the racial/ethnic composition of the position is taken into account, especially when considering employment trends within Alameda County. As table 1.3 illustrates, White non-Hispanic men's share of transit operator positions decreased from 30 percent in 1980 to 10 percent between 2006 and 2010, while African American men's share decreased from 33 percent to 15 percent. Alameda County's Latino American and Asian American men and women experienced substantial gains in this position. With Latino American men's share of the position outpacing African American men's share by 2010, Latino American women's share of transit operator position in Alameda County grew from 2 percent in 1980 to 8 percent 2000 and 13 percent between 2006 and 2010. Finally, table 1.3 illustrates that African American women currently hold the largest share of transit

Table 1.3 Percentage of State of California and Alameda County transit operators by gender and race, 1980, 1990, 2000, and 2006–2010

Race		1980		1990		2000		2006–2010	
		CA	Alameda	CA	Alameda	CA	Alameda	CA	Alameda
Total	Men	62	74	58	57	56	58	59	48
	Women	38	26	42	43	44	42	41	52
White–non-Hispanic	Men	35	30	26	11	21	7	16	10
	Women	26	13	24	11	21	13	15	4
Black–non-Hispanic	Men	17	33	16	37	12	31	12	15
	Women	7	11	10	19	11	22	12	28
Latin American	Men	8	5	12	3	16	6	23	28
	Women	4	2	7	2	10	8	12	13
Asian American	Men	2	6	3	5	4.40	0	7	9
	Women	0.50	0.30	0	0	0.20	0	0.90	2
Native American	Men	0.34	0	1	1	0.20	0.70	0.40	0
	Women	0.68	0	1	0	0.10	0.40	0.20	0

Source: U.S. Census Bureau, *Census 1990 and 2000 special tabulations for the State of California*; U.S. Census Bureau, *Equal Employment Opportunity (EEO) Tabulation 2006–2010 (5-Year ACS Data)* (Washington, D.C.: U.S. Census Bureau, 1990 and 2000), 75 and 78; U.S. Census Bureau, *EEO Special File Summarized Occupational Categories by Race/Hispanic Origin and Sex for Alameda County* (Washington, D.C.: U.S. Census Bureau, 1980), 79; U.S. Census Bureau, *EEO Special File Summarized Occupational Categories by Race/Hispanic Origin and Sex for California* (Washington, D.C.: U.S. Census Bureau, 1980), 79.

operator positions in Alameda County. While White non-Hispanic women's share of this occupation declined substantially from 13 percent to 4 percent between 2006 and 2010, African American women's share of Alameda County transit operator jobs rose from 11 percent in 1980 to 28 percent between 2006 and 2010.

Study Design

In order to uncover the social, economic, and bureaucratic aspects of African American women transit operator's work opportunity within AC Transit between 1974 and 2009, I rely on two types of data: archival data from various archives and the U.S. Census Bureau and interviews with African American women transit operators. The archive data on AC Transit helped inform my understanding of how changes in the labor process and worker solidarity influenced the bargaining potential of transit operators employed by transit districts between 1975 and 2009. I secured data from the Federal Employment Practice Committee Collection and the Records of the War Manpower Commission housed at the Pacific region's National Archives and Records Administration near San Francisco, California. These archives revealed a great deal about how World War II–era race relations manifested in the East Bay and how these racial antagonisms influenced efforts to maintain a segregated local labor market within the transit industry. These archives document state and federal efforts made to improve working conditions and race relations within the East Bay transit industry and other industries.

In addition, I gathered historical materials from a collection located at Labor Archives and Research Center at San Francisco State University that documents the activities and motives of the ATU 192, which is the labor union that represents nonsupervisory AC Transit workers. I used the Sam Kagel Collection as well as the Amalgamated Transit Union, Local 192 (Oakland, California) Records. The Sam Kagel Collection contains key arbitration decisions as well as materials documenting the relationship between the union, workers, and AC Transit. The ATU 192 Collection helps uncover the activities of ATU and its members from 1930 to 2004 and provides some insight into transit employees' working conditions. Documents gathered from this archive include incoming and outgoing correspondence, reports, newsletters from factions that formed within the union to protest racial prejudice within the union ranks, correspondence from high-ranking union officials about the racial tensions within the union movement, financial records, bargaining files, and arbitration and mediation decisions. The records in this archive showed trends of passengers abusing transit operators and peculiar[50] patterns embedded in the discipline write-ups between 1984 and 1987. This archive also contains key grievance cases and arbitration decisions, as well as materials documenting the relationship between the union and AC Transit.

I used trade journals and public records to help describe hiring patterns and other important factors shaping labor relations within AC Transit throughout the period of study. For instance, in addition to combing through more than twenty lawsuits filed against AC Transit during the period of study, I examined AC Transit's *Annual Reports* from 1961 to 1988 to document claims of race and gender discrimination. These reports helped me illustrate rider trends and how federal grants and other revenue streams were utilized by the firm. Moreover, these reports provide insight into composition shifts in AC Transit's management team and board of directors, as well as its record with national awards and efforts to keep pace with national transit trends.

I also compiled AC Transit's list and pictures of new hires as documented in its publication *Transit Times* to illustrate AC Transit's hiring and placement patterns two years before African American women began being hired to work as transit operators and for several years after this dramatic change. From these reports, I was able to identify the race, gender, division placement, and year of hire for 650 full-time employees hired between 1972 and 1978. I was able to document the degree to which AC Transit participated in reconstituting inequality within the workplace by way of job placement within its four divisions: Emeryville, Richmond, East Oakland, and Newark (now Hayward).

Lastly, I secured AC Transit's drug-testing program data and audits of the program that were conducted by the Federal Transit Administration (FTA) between 1996 and 2010. It was imperative to secure this information in order to fact-check or triangulate the information received from transit operator interviewees, who consistently reported that the random drug-testing program within AC Transit was far from random. Workers claimed that the tests were predictable in their capacity to single out high-seniority African American transit operators and supervisors. I was happy to secure the FTA data for this analysis, not only because it substantiated the workers claims, but also because, when exposed, the patterns of disparate surveillance and punishment that emerge in FTA data may inspire other researchers to examine common, devastating worker abuses in the neoliberal era.

In-Depth Interviewing

After reading trade journals and newspaper accounts of transit operators' working conditions, I thought that I had my act together. I thought that I knew what mattered in the transit workplace—until I spoke with a few workers. I quickly realized that my questions didn't need to drive our conversation. Instead, I positioned myself to allow their insight about their experiences to drive my inquiry. I eventually had to throw out my original questionnaire: its content was obsolete, derived from the transit journals and complicating my capacity to take into account the situated experiences of workers. My revised questionnaire was designed to capture how my interviewees related to their workplace environment and the strategies they used to navigate the opportunities available to them. Consistent with feminist critiques of qualitative research methods that stress the importance of encouraging egalitarian relationships grounded in trust, I used the "active" approach as my primary interviewing method.

In order to identify workers who would allow me to interview and observe them, I attended local labor union meetings in my capacity as a graduate student researcher employed by the University of California, Berkeley's Labor Center. My initial interviews were with union representatives and supervisors, who helped me gain access to transit operator interviewees through direct introductions. I also was successful in securing transit operator interviewees by catching them on break at BART stations. Much of my success in securing transit operators on break depended on my ability to gain their trust with a quick, honest, and sincere request for their time. I was warned by my initial interviewees that it would be hard for me to find other respondents: while transit operators may seem open to the passengers they serve, they were, I was told, incredibly guarded and needed reassurance that I was not working on behalf of AC Transit, which monitors workers through audio and visual technology and passengers hired to observe transit operators' adherence to company policy while on the road. In total, I interviewed fifteen African American women of varying family backgrounds and ages who worked in various capacities at AC Transit. Thirteen of the respondents were transit operators, and two were supervisors with extensive transit operating experience with AC Transit.

I asked workers how they gained access to their transit operating jobs and the degree to which they felt marginalized at work. I also probed for feedback regarding perceived changes in job status and quality of conditions during their tenure. The interviews, conducted at the District Four Headquarters and at various BART locations in the San Francisco Bay Area between 2005 and 2006, lasted forty-five minutes to 1.5 hours and were supplemented by demographic surveys completed by transit operator interviewees. Finally, I rode with some of the respondents on their routes to observe their interactions with colleagues and patrons. I recorded the interviews, changed interviewees' names to protect their confidentiality, and transcribed the recorded exchanges. I analyzed the data by reading (and rereading) my transcripts and employing inductive coding techniques that enabled me to identify important themes related to understanding my respondents' workplace experiences throughout the period of study.

Given my multilayered approach to understanding African American women's progress as transit operators and the work/life conflicts that emerged, I chose to situate this analysis within a regional economy and occupation in which workers have a long history of fighting for—and winning—many rewards and rights. Against the backdrop of widespread demographic shifts in a coveted occupation, I explored the social, economic, and bureaucratic sources of employment (in)security within AC Transit in the San Francisco Bay Area for various reasons. First, when African American women began working for AC Transit, this mass transit provider was the highest paying transit employer in the nation and nationally recognized for the maintenance of its fleet for over a decade. However, despite this history, public commentary on the conditions of work within AC Transit suggests that circumstances have soured and work conditions have devolved since the mid-1970s. This study chronicles how this employer and union, ATU 192, the first labor organization in the nation to negotiate equal pay for women, responded to external pressure to hire African American women workers.

My second reason for exploring work progress within this San Francisco Bay Area transit workplace is an interest in expanding what we know about the nature of employment relations within this local labor market. Given decades of exemplary research on the variations in the configurations of inequality across geographic boundaries, we know a great deal about how opportunity structures and workplace returns vary among cities like Rust-Belt Detroit; Atlanta, with its strong service-based economy and persistent Black/White segregation; Boston, a rising technology center whose social and political structure is complicated by the arrival of Asian and Latino immigrants; and Los Angeles, a destination for new immigrants that continues to thrive due to the growth in high-tech, finance, service, and tourist industry jobs.[51] However, the structure of opportunity within low-skilled workers residing in the East Bay area, especially in the neoliberal context, has received limited attention.

The San Francisco metropolitan area provides a suitable location from which to explore shifts in job progress because it has undergone a substantial reversal of fortunes. In the postindustrial era, geographer Richard A. Walker characterizes California as a "Frankensteinian laboratory of modern hopes and failures," despite the state's liberal labor history and its continuing support of public sector unions.[52] Similar to other blue-collar and semiskilled occupations throughout this country, there also have been substantial shifts with regard to sex categories across those industries that are the largest employers of African American workers in the Bay Area. The San Francisco Bay Area transportation industry, ranked third on the list of the ten industries with the largest number of African American workers in 2000, saw its percentage of women workers increase from 9 percent in 1970 to 28 percent in 2000.[53]

This case study provides an opportunity to explore the underlying mechanisms driving the patterns observed in the statistical analyses, especially as they relate to the downward shifts in the structure of opportunities available to low-skilled workers. While much of our public discourse about mobility focuses on worker characteristics and much of our academic and policy discourse focuses on overall changes in the economy, I will show that looking more closely at the mesolevel—of the employer and the union—yields a richer understanding of workplace progress. It also shows how racial and gender stratification is maintained, despite the implementation of affirmative action goals.

2

From Exclusion to Selective Inclusion

Pre-1975 Employment Trends in the Transit Industry

Helen Capehart, a thirty-six-year-old African American woman with a four-year college education, applied for a conductorette position in November 1944 but was told at the Los Angeles Transit Company Hiring Hall that she did not qualify because she lived in Watts, which would require a long commute to work. Two months later, on referral from the U.S. Employment Service, Mrs. Capehart applied for the position again after moving to Los Angeles, only to find that the company did not have any openings for the conductorette position. The interviewer mentioned that he would send a card once a position emerged, but Mrs. Capehart never received notice of an opening. She filed a complaint with the Fair Employment Practice Committee (FEPC), indicating her belief that their refusal to hire her was based on her race.[1] FEPC records reveal that during the World War II era, the Los Angeles Transit Company and other transportation firms were in the habit of turning away workers of color, employing excuses based on job-seekers' external characteristics or circumstances and by claiming that no positions other than that of car cleaners were available, even when the U.S. Employment Service had referred these job-seekers and the transit companies were actively advertising for trainmen, conductors, mechanics, and mechanics' helpers.[2]

Helen Capehart's story echoes in the experiences of many other women, including Mary Ruth Franklin of Los Angeles, who began working for the Los Angeles Transit Company as a car cleaner in December 1944. She wanted to secure a conductorette job but was told that she was too heavy for the job. At that time, Franklin was a 5' 6.5" twenty-eight-year-old high school graduate weighing 170 pounds.[3] After deciding to work as a car cleaner, she learned that she would be required to join the union within thirty days of starting her job in order to qualify for the $7-per-month membership rate. If she failed to become a union member within the required number of days, she would be forced to pay $27 every month for membership dues. She ended up filing a complaint with the FEPC because the union had refused to accept her as a member and she still had not received a transfer to the conductorette position. This time, J. W. Prutsman, a business agent for the Rails Department, informed her that if she still desired a transfer, she would need to appeal to the personnel manager at 1056 S. Broadway. The personnel manager told her that in addition to her weight, her less than perfect eyesight excluded her from consideration. While acknowledging that she wore glasses, Franklin contended that she could see well with and without her glasses. Due to the Los Angeles Transit Company's persistent denial of Franklin's request for a transfer, she contacted the FEPC, expressing her concern that the refusal was because she is an African American.[4]

While transit management explained its refusal to hire African Americans on the basis of the public's disproval of African Americans in certain positions and their presumed inability to function in public capacities, racial antagonisms within labor unions and long-standing disputes between labor unions and management often negatively affected the employment opportunities of African American women workers like Franklin and Capehart. Just before receiving a directive from FEPC, transit companies such as the Los Angeles Transportation Company decided in 1943 to take a stance against discrimination by posting notices on all company bulletin boards alerting workers that opposition to the hiring and training of African Americans was against company and union laws. Contrary to the transit company's public stance against discrimination in the workplace, top union officials representing the Los Angeles local of American Federation of Labor's Amalgamated Association of Street and Electric Railway and Motor Coach Employees of America previously made attempts to delay efforts to hire African Americans by actively campaigning against their employment within the workplace. When two African American men were hired at a bus station as mechanics' helpers in 1943, eighty White workers responded to this development by engaging in a work stoppage that lasted two hours. In response to the reactions of White workers, management ordered that the African American workers be sent back to their original positions in the firm. All was well until management attempted to promote a few African American workers several days later. In response to management's push to desegregate the workplace, the White workers responded with another work stoppage. Since the company did not have much luck in dealing with the labor union on its own, it requested state help. Unfortunately, the War Labor Board and the Labor Department Conciliation Service took no action on the employer's referral.[5]

Though the War Labor Board and the Labor Department Conciliation Service did not take action, the city government of Los Angeles did. It intervened in this situation directly, but the effort failed because union officials refused to negotiate further with the company and proclaimed that they would not obey any directive to support the employment and promotion of African American workers. Finally, in August 1944, the company and the union decided to comply with the government directive to integrate the workplace. The impetus for the change was falling into the awkward position of having to explain the controversy surrounding the employment and promotion of African American workers to officials of the city of Los Angeles at a conference chaired by the FEPC.[6]

Although the Los Angeles Transit Company agreed to integrate its workplace, the FEPC records brim with complaints of African American women and men attempting to secure jobs within the firm. Race-based exclusion from the transit workplace is not specific to the Los Angeles area. If fact, employment discrimination against African Americans was rampant in the transit industry at large. This chapter documents the history of African American women workers in the transit industry between 1940 and the mid-1970s. In addition to arguing that the industry underutilized African Americans, I cite a variety of East Bay area African American women workers' experiences attempting to gain access to transit operator jobs in order to reveal a highly inequitable structure of opportunity.

Pre-1970 History of Employment Trends among African Americans as Transit Operators in the San Francisco Bay Area

Just after the San Francisco earthquake and fire of 1906, the population of Alameda County doubled from 130,000 to 246,000 between 1900 and 1910, while the population of Contra Costa County experienced a similar increase from 18,000 to 32,000 during the same period.[7] Public transportation by companies like Southern Pacific, its subsidiary, Interurban Electric Company, and Key System played a crucial role in facilitating the population growth in these eleven cities that make up the east shore of the San Francisco Bay. Rail, streetcar, and bus services transported patrons traveling from home to work and back, who worked for a variety of establishments ranging from paper mills and steel plants and power plants to the more developed areas of Alameda and Contra Costa counties like the harbor facilities as well as the business and commercial centers.

During World War II, many cities in the United States underwent a transformation as tens of thousands of African American migrants poured in from southern states. In Richmond, California, the number of African Americans increased from 270 in 1940 to 10,000 in 1945. The African American population in Oakland increased from 8,472 to more than 37,000 during this period. The East Bay African American population increased by more than 227 percent, replacing Asian immigrants as the largest racial minority in the area. A trigger of this influx was Franklin Roosevelt's Executive Order 8802 barring racial discrimination in defense industries and defense contracts, which opened up new job opportunities for African Americans. Many of the migrants, from states such as Mississippi, Texas, Arkansas, and Oklahoma, were joining East Bay relatives in West Oakland or responding to recruitment efforts by area companies seeking cheap labor. Migrants came looking for jobs, but they also came in hopes of securing social rights.[8]

Viewed as undesirable guest workers by both White and Black East Bay residents, African American migrants faced an uphill battle. White migrants from west central states could use whiteness as a currency in their transition, while migrant African Americans had to contend with intense racial tensions and restrictions ranging from race-motivated street fights and racial barriers to federally funded war housing to extensive employment discrimination. Although established and migrant African Americans differed in many ways, established African American residents eventually found themselves subjected to racial restrictions and hostility as well as labor issues that peaked as the result of demographic changes in the East Bay and the white population's efforts to maintain White privilege in the area. Housing was racially segregated, and African Americans lost access to public spaces such as bars, hotels, and restaurants as White business owners started refusing to serve African American patrons. Employment opportunities were especially limited. Employers avoided hiring African American workers, while labor unions such as the Boilermakers and the ATU notoriously refused to extend union membership to these workers. Unions led by White ethnic groups typically protected White privilege by negotiating closed-shop agreements with Bay Area employers or setting up Jim Crow auxiliaries that excluded dues-paying African American workers from union elections and policy decisions.

African American women workers fared better in the East Bay than they had in the South, but they still tended to work in the area of personal service, occupying the least desirable jobs with the lowest pay. Their relative status compared to other workers remained the same due to race and gender discrimination.[9] Defense industries tended to hire and train White women to work the safest and best-paying jobs available to women. For instance, 63 percent of African American women worked as welder trainees and laborers, while most White women workers were employed as inspectors, ship-fitters, machinists, tank sealers, and painters. Only 6 percent of White women were laborers, 9 percent welder trainees, and 9 percent electrician trainees.[10]

By 1945, African Americans faced a great deal of hardship when the war boom was over and employment opportunities evaporated. After experiencing postwar unemployment, most African American men secured semiskilled or unskilled industrial positions that included warehouse work, construction, packing, longshore, and primary metals production, while those engaged in service work found employment as janitors, cooks, bartenders, porters, and parking attendants.[11] African American male workers earned less than White men both during and after the war.

African American women's employment circumstances were similar to African American men's labor experiences. By 1945, most African American women had lost their defense jobs, despite the Women's Bureau's finding that 95 percent of non-White women hoped to continue working.[12] While African American women did eventually secure other jobs, they continued to occupy the lowest rungs of the occupational hierarchy as unskilled factory or service workers. For instance, in 1948, only one-fifth of Bay Area African American women secured managerial, clerical, or professional jobs, the type of work that represents three-fourths of all Bay Area women workers.[13] By 1960, over 50 percent of African American women workers in the Bay Area labored in service occupations as custodians, nurse's aides, and cooks, compared to 17 percent of all Bay Area women.[14]

Still, in 1945, West Oakland boomed with women's clubs, lodges, and churches, while places such as the Seventh Street commercial district thrived with African American–owned businesses and office buildings, including Slim Jenkin's jazz club on Seventh and Wood streets. This and other community-oriented establishments helped southern migrants in this district develop a sense of community. Despite this growing sense of community, residential segregation continued to limit African Americans severely by restricting them to substandard housing with high rents. A 1944 report by Sociologist Charles S. Johnson notes that "27 percent to 66 percent of Negro housing [was] substandard. Five times as many Negroes in Japtown as were previously . . . [and that] 43 percent of families [had] no bathrooms."[15]

Like the African American migrants who settled in Los Angeles, African American migrants to the East Bay area, who primarily came with an eighth-grade education from Texas, Louisiana, and Oklahoma, found job opportunities in war plants, while other employers generally overlooked these workers. While some large Oakland firms such as the Southern Pacific Company, the Moore Drydock Company, and the U.S. Navy Supply Base employed a large segment of non-White workers, other firms such as the Bethlehem Alameda Shipyards, the InterUrban Express Company, the Hurley Marine Works, and Key System Transit Lines hired only a few African Americans in the year 1944—or in some cases, none at all.

Workers of East Bay area firms filed various charges of discrimination based on religion and nationality, but, the vast majority of discrimination charges came from African Americans who reported that they experienced discrimination when attempting to secure employment. Fifty-nine percent of the 453 complaints submitted to the San Francisco Regional FEPC office between 1944 and 1945 and 40 percent of the 360 complaints in Los Angeles related to a refusal to hire. Most of the complaints filed with the Los Angeles Regional FEPC office by hired workers concerned discriminatory discharges and inequitable working conditions. Specifically, 13 percent of the complaints in San Francisco related to discriminatory discharges, while 18 percent of the complaints involved allegations of workplace discrimination, and 10 percent of complaints related to discrimination by labor unions.[16]

Bay Area Employment Restrictions in the Transit Industry

In lieu of filing formal complaints concerning the actions of employers and unions, many East Bay area workers who faced limited employment opportunities during the World War II era wrote letters to the FEPC and in many cases directly to President Franklin D. Roosevelt detailing the nature of race-based exclusion in the transit workplace. Letters poured in from workers like San Francisco resident and Market Street Railroad worker Spencer O. Rogers, pleading for direct action.

August 26, 1943

Dear Mr. Roosevelt-
Railroad employers . . . refuse to hire Negros irregardless of their skill . . . . I will quote a conversation between the Market Street Railroad and a Negro delegation [where] the management's answer [for not hiring Blacks] was "we don't have toilet facilities for your race and so we can't hire them."

August 28, 1943

To the President of the U.S.

Dear Sir:
I am only a motorman on the Municipal R.R. of S. F. . . . . We are facing a critical shortage on the cars here . . . [but] recalcitrant employers are refusing to hire efficient Negro help . . . . [They are] helping Hitler by refusing to hire willing and skilled work-ers of the Negro race . . . . Transportation is the same as the circulation of the blood and is vital to win the War. Why did your famous Order 8802 stop at defense industries and not include industries essential to defense?

Spencer O. Rogers 3109 Geary San Francisco, Calif.

Despite persistent complaints from workers like Spencer Rogers,[17] non-White employment in the East Bay did not improve within firms, including Southern Pacific Company and Municipal Railway in San Francisco as well as Key System Transit Lines.[18] Although many of these workers had, according to the Manpower Program for the Local Transit Industry, "proved themselves capable of performing transit jobs with varying skill requirements when given an opportunity," East Bay area transit employers typically restricted them to jobs requiring little or no skill because management and labor did not want to modify existing policies and practices used to exclude these workers.[19] Some transit com-panies began hiring women to perform jobs typically held by men. How-ever, Department of Defense Transportation inspectors also discovered that many more employers were, as noted in the "Manpower Program in the Local Transit Industry" report, "still skeptical as to the ability of women to perform jobs other than clerical, [while] some local labor organizations have hampered the employment of women by failing to permit relaxations of working rules or policies, such as modification of seniority rules and adjustment of work assignments."[20]

Since the city of Oakland was flourishing during the World War II era, some people thought that the social and community transformations would eventually extend to the economic sphere and that wartime conditions would bring new and better employment options to African Americans and other marginalized groups in the area, but they were wrong. They were especially wrong in the case of East Bay area transportation firms such as Key System Transit Lines. During this time, Key System confronted mounting difficulties stemming from its inability to maintain its operating equipment. During rush hours, passengers frequently had to wait for seriously delayed coaches and rail units thanks to the fact that 31 percent of the company's equipment was in need of repairs and was not in use.[21] Although Bay Area companies such as Key System lacked workers, most transportation companies still made efforts to avoid hiring both African American men and women. In response to Key System's dire need for mechanics, Berkeley, California, resident Lige Webb, who had nine years of experience as a mechanic and had been employed as a mechanic at Becker's Tire Company, applied for a mechanic position in August and September 1945. However, Key Transit refused to hire Webb, claiming they did not have any openings at the time. At the suggestion of the Oakland U.S. Employment Service, Webb submitted a complaint to the FEPC, alleging that Key System discriminated against him by refusing to hire him due to his race.[22] Despite efforts by the War Manpower Commission and the Committee for Fair Employment Practices to lessen opposition to racial minorities, full community support for employing African Americans and other racial minorities in war effort jobs was slow to emerge. Instead of hiring workers like Webb during the wartime era, Bay Area employers were swept up in the hysteria and opposition that emerged regarding African American workers' migration to the West Coast. This contestation affected every aspect of African American life in the East Bay, from where one was free to reside and worship to what was available in terms of public bathrooms and schools as well as employment opportunities.

Key System's refusal to hire African Americans coupled with the union's racial restrictions on membership ensured that Key System remained segregated during the World War II period—and the union, ATU 192, played no small part in this outcome. Key Systems had entered into its first contract with ATU 192 on January 1, 1926. From the start of this labor management relationship until 1941, Local 192 exercised its power through a "for cause" provision to bar African Americans from employment with Key System. In other words, if Key System wished to refuse employment or union membership to candidates, the company had to provide a specific cause for the refusal. While negotiating the 1941–1942 contract, Local 192 made efforts to do away with the "for clause" provision in favor of "the right to reject any application for membership."[23] This initial attempt to gain absolute control over the employment process failed because Key System did not want to concede to the union's demands. However, like other transit employers, Key System also wanted to avoid any work stoppages or strikes inspired by racist sentiment, so rather than granting Local 192 absolute control, Key System eventually agreed to require that new employees become members of ATU 192 as a condition of employment, stating in the contract that "all employees covered by this agreement must become members of the Association and remain members in good standing as a condition precedent to continued employment. . . . The Association reserves the right to reject application for membership in accordance with the laws of the Association."[24] By 1944, Local 192 won the right to reject potential employees without restrictions.

ATU 192's pressure to establish explicit control over hiring practices escalated in response to demands placed on employers to hire African American labor during World War II. Prior to this time, there had not been a need to gain control over hiring practices because White male laborers did not have to compete with African American workers for positions within many privately owned transit firms since. This lack of competition was, of course, because employers like Key System typically avoided hiring African Americans altogether, while others excluded them from the higher paying and more prestigious positions set aside for White workers.

During the pressures of wartime and federal measures to integrate the workforce, even labor shortages pushed unions to become more aggressive in their opposition to efforts threatening to disturb the racial status quo. For instance, while Key System and other transit employers such as the Los Angeles Transportation Company continued to work with labor unions to avoid placing African American workers in coveted positions during wartime, these firms faced steep challenges stemming from labor shortages and complaints of poor service. In 1943, Key System spent $52,000 on an advertising campaign designed to recruit and retain workers. However, despite its need to secure workers, the company did not attempt to desegregate its workforce. Between 1941 and 1945, Key System referred 27,000 White applicants to the union for approval, but the firm did not make any African American membership referrals until 1945 when it attempted to hire eight African Americans. Based on its closed-shop agreement with Key System, Local 192 denied membership to each African American the company had referred.[25]

The Role of the FEPC in Breaking Racial Barriers within Key System

Ongoing discrimination against African American job applicants within Key System and the ATU 192 became a public concern when, in March 1945, the FEPC began investigating claims of discrimination at Key System. Despite the company's denial of racial discrimination and the ATU 192's stance that its practices were for the purposes of protecting its members' wishes, U.S. Attorney Bruce Hunt charged both of these organizations with refusing to hire qualified African American applicants and denying membership on the basis of their race. When asked by the FEPC to explain Local 192's stance on African American workers, ATU 192 president Alfred Brown claimed there had been no good reason to employ African Americans as operators because they had not been needed. At the FEPC's hearings regarding Key System's employment practices, Brown explained that a union subcommittee had denied membership to African American candidates because "they won't accept a Negro." As a precaution, just prior to voting on an applicant's petition for membership, Brown stated that he would perform his "duty" to the union by alerting the membership of the candidate's racial status as an African American. Because of this practice, the union routinely approved membership for White workers while denying membership to their Black counterparts. In an attempt to clarify Local 192's motivations for excluding African Americans from membership, one FEPC representative asked, "In other words, Mr. Brown, if a man is colored, you would not pass him merely because he's colored?" Brown responded by saying "That's right. I know my membership."[26]

Notwithstanding the public attention generated by the FEPC, the organization's efforts to adjust both Key System's hiring practices and the union's stance on African American workers were overwhelmingly unsuccessful. Attorney Hunt contended that the hearings fell apart well before ATU 192 withdrew from the hearing. In his opinion, efforts to desegregate the operator and mechanic positions within Key System failed because Key System and the union had never intended to cooperate with the FEPC's probe into the company's hiring practices, nor were they willing to produce the records necessary for the FEPC to investigate the allegations. Attorney Hunt came to believe that the company and the union had prepared their cases together, planning to deflect charges by contesting the FEPC's jurisdiction and authority despite the glaring evidence of discrimination in company records—and the evidence was obvious: the union's newspaper even included anti-Black jokes and stories that fed racial fears of Black men victimizing White women operators. In addition to the union, Key System was not shy in their criticism of the FEPC's efforts. In legal correspondence, Key System characterized the committee's representatives with the exception of Regional FEPC Director Harry Kingman, a personal friend of the company's president, Alfred J. Lundberg, as an army of individuals who did not set out to encourage understanding, but to "achieve some kind of technical triumph . . . and to create as much dissension as possible."[27]

While the refusal by union officials and company management to participate in the FEPC's investigation certainly influenced the agency's ability to encourage shifts in the racial composition of operating jobs, the FEPC's own weaknesses also stalled the progress of African American workers in transit occupations. The FEPC was contending at the time with an internal reorganization. This, combined with consistent opposition from interest groups, left the FEPC as Weaver contended "hanging by a slender thread" and lacking the ability to enforce its orders.[28]

In addition, the FEPC's compromised authority in the Bay Area reflected delays in its investigations of discrimination cases and its practice of selective enforcement. Several letters between the FEPC and War Manpower Commission illustrate the latter agency's concern with the FEPC's practice of closing cases due to the lack of jurisdiction. The FEPC developed a pattern of investigating the cases involving discrimination within war production industries while rejecting cases involving essential activities concerned with and contributing to war production and civilian requirements.[29] Acting Director Sam Kagel of the War Manpower

Commission in turn refused to respond to complaints of discrimination because of the FEPC's failure to issue appropriate directives that would enable the War Manpower Commission to employ sanctions against a discriminatory employer and/or union. In discrimination cases involving the Richmond Shipyards, Kagel refused to take direct action. Most notably, he refused to take direct action against the Boilermakers Locals 5, 6, 39, and 513 until the FEPC charged the company or the unions with discrimination and issued directives to the organizations engaged in discriminatory employment and training practices.[30] Special arrangements between the Richmond Shipyards and unions representing boilermakers, electricians, machinists, sheet Metal Workers, steamfitters, and helpers ensured the exclusion of African Americans from certain positions, upgrades, supervisory roles, and training opportunities.

Key System represents just one of many resistant Bay Area firms that delayed African American employment even in the face of post–World War II labor shortages caused by White workers "jumping the streetcars" for better prospects in the shipyards. As a result of firm and union opposition to desegregating the workplace, Key System Transit Lines did not employ African Americans as operators or mechanics during wartime. ATU 192 continued to successfully bar African American workers from employment through closed-shop agreements with employers even after the Taft-Hartley Act in 1947 prohibited the closed shop.[31]

Shifts in racialized hiring did eventually emerge in the East Bay area but not without significant battles between transit employers and African American leaders. Efforts to desegregate the workforce at Key System began with conversations with C. L. Dellums, a business agent for the Brotherhood of Sleeping Car Porters, and peaked with a FEPC investigation and activism by the Alameda County Branch of the National Association for the Advancement of Colored People. Only after seven years of protest did Key System integrate its workforce. The company hired its first African American male transit operator in 1951, motivated largely by the National Association for the Advancement of Colored People's threat to boycott Key System as well its persistent appeals to the Public Utilities Commission to deny the company's request to reduce service due to labor shortages—labor shortages that were, of course, the direct result of Key System's refusal to hire qualified African American applicants.[32]

Key System Transit's reluctance to hire African American male transit operators mirrored the industry-wide treatment of African American male and female workers. Table 2.1 demonstrates the urban transit

Table 2.1 Employment by race and sex in the urban transit industry, 1940–1960

Year	All Employees % African American	Men % African American	Female % African American
1940	3	3	3
1950	6	6	7
1960	11	11	8

Source: U.S. Census of Population, *The Labor Force, U.S. Summary*, Volume 3 (Washington, D.C.: U.S. Census Bureau, 1940), table 76; U.S. Census of Population, *Characteristics of the Population, Part 1, U.S. Summary*, Volume 2 (Washington, D.C.: U.S. Census Bureau, 1950), table 133; U.S. Census of Population, *U.S. Summary, Detailed Characteristics*, PC (1) 1D (Washington, D.C.: U.S. Census Bureau, 1960), table 213.

industry's long history of underutilizing African American workers. In 1940, African American workers held 3 percent of all positions. By 1960, both African American women and men experienced a net increase in their share of urban transit industry jobs. While African American men held 11 percent of the jobs available to male workers, by 1960, African American women constituted 8 percent of the urban transit industry's female workforce.

African Americans' best opportunity to secure work in the urban transit industry was in the South, as illustrated in table 2.2, which presents the percentage of African Americans employed in 1940, 1950, and 1960 by region. African American men's share of jobs in the urban transit industry in the South doubled from 8 percent in 1940 to 16 percent in 1960. African American women's share of urban transit jobs in the South increased from 8 percent in 1940 to 14 percent in 1960. The presence of African American men and women in the urban transit workforce of the West was conspicuously low between 1940 and 1960. African American men's share of positions within this industry grew from 1 percent in 1940 to 6 percent in 1960. Meanwhile, although African American women held 4 percent of the jobs in the urban transit industry in 1940, their share of jobs in this industry decreased to 2 percent by 1960.

Table 2.3 illustrates the percentage of African American men and women workers employed as transit operators in selected cities in 1945. In order to observe the relationship between a city's demographic makeup and African American workers' share of transit operator positions in the area, this table also reports the percentage of African Americans residing

Table 2.2 Employment by region, race, and sex in the urban transit
industry, 1940–1960

Region	Year	All Employees % African American	Men % African American	Female % African American
West	1940	1	1	4
	1950	4	4	3
	1960	5	6	2
Midwest	1940	2	2	2
	1950	5	5	5
	1960	9	10	4
Northeast	1940	3	3	2
	1950	6	6	5
	1960	10	10	9
South	1940	8	8	8
	1950	10	9	12
	1960	16	16	14

Source: U.S. Census of Population, *The Labor Force, U.S. Summary*, Volume 3 (Washington, D.C.: U.S. Census Bureau, 1940), table 77; U.S. Census of Population, *Characteristics of the Population, Part 1, U.S. Summary*, Volume 2 (Washington, D.C.: U.S. Census Bureau, 1950), table 161; U.S. Census of Population, *U.S. Summary, Detailed Characteristics*, PC (1) 1D (Washington, D.C.: U.S. Census Bureau, 1960), Table 260.

in the selected cities. In 1945, most African American male workers were excluded from transit operator positions. As table 2.3 demonstrates, in selected American cities, their share of this position was less than 10 percent, with the exception of Detroit, where African American men held 21 percent of the transit operator positions. Meanwhile, African American women held far fewer transit operator positions in 1945. African American women workers held no more than 3 percent of the transit operator positions in Detroit, while holding 1 percent of these positions in New York and San Francisco.

Table 2.3 suggests that urban transit industry hiring trends were independent of the number of African Americans residing in a given community. Data on transit operator positions in 1945 demonstrates that these race- and gender-specific hiring trends were fairly consistent. This evidence also suggests that the practice of excluding African American workers from the transit operator position was a widespread industry norm.

Table 2.3 Urban transit industry African American operators in selected cities and other occupations, January 1945

| City | Total Operators | Percentage of African American Transit Operators | | % African Americans in Area in 1950 |
		Male	Female	
Chicago	13,236	1	*	10.70
Cleveland	3,287	6	0	10.50
Detroit	4,874	21	3	12
Los Angeles	1,670	2	1	8.40
New York	12,554	7	1	7
San Francisco	2,455	2	—	7

* No African American women hired as transit operators in area.
Source: Philips W. Jeffress, *The Negro in the Urban Transit Industry* (Philadelphia: University of Pennsylvania Press, 1970), tables 10, 11, and 18, pp. 26–27, 56.

By 1966, circumstances had changed considerably for African American male workers, but circumstances had not changed much among African American women workers. Table 2.4 illustrates the percentage of African Americans employed within the urban transit industry by sex and occupational group. In this year, African American male workers filled 20 percent of all operative positions (primarily consisting of transit operators). While African American male and female workers had different experiences within the urban transit industry, they shared in common a disproportionate presence in service positions. In 1966, African American male workers held 35 percent and 27 percent of the laborer and service positions, respectively. Meanwhile, African American women workers held 2 percent of all service occupations. Table 2.4 reveals that among all women hired for service jobs, African American women held 54 percent of laborer jobs and 35 percent of the service positions, which primarily consisted of bus cleaning jobs. African American women constituted 42 percent of the women hired to clean the buses and street cars. You will not be surprised to learn from this table that in 1966, African American women had not gained access to managerial and professional positions in the urban transit industry.

Table 2.4 Percentage of African Americans employed by urban transit industry by sex and occupational group, 1966

Occupational Group	All Employees % Black Men	All Employees % Black Women	Male Workers % Black	Women Workers % Black
Officials and managers	2	—	2	-
Professionals	2	—	3	-
Technicians	3	0	3	7
Sales workers	8	1	10	8
Office and clerical	2	2	3	4
Total white collar	4	1	5	5
Craft workers	5	0.02	5	4
Operatives	20	0.18	20	10
Total blue collar	16	0.13	16	9
Laborers	35	3	37	54
Service workers	27	1	28	35
Total pink collar	30	2	31	42

Source: Philips W. Jeffress, *The Negro in the Urban Transit Industry* (Philadelphia: University of Pennsylvania Press, 1970), table 20, p. 62.

Declining Fortunes Lead to Increased Employment Opportunity for African American and Women Workers: Management's Shift from Private to Public

Over time, the populations within Alameda and Contra Costa Counties continued to expand. By 1957, Alameda and Contra Costa Counties made up nearly one-half of the East Bay population, a shift from representing one-fourth of the area in 1900. However, despite expansions in East Bay industries and the population, shifts in the nature of East Bay area public transportation emerged after World War II when the demand for public transportation declined. By 1956, per capita transit riding in the area was among the lowest in the country and local transit riding in the East Bay declined to less than forty-three million riders, 38 percent of the peak this metropolitan area reached in 1945. Although the opening of the Bay Bridge in 1937 provided a boost to transbay travel and patrons increasingly utilized the transit services available in Contra Costa County, transbay mass transit trips declined substantially from eighty-one million in 1946 to nine million in 1957.[33]

By 1948, Key System Transit Lines had converted the last electric streetcar lines to bus routes and was forced to cut service and increase fares due to declining patronage. Its public reputation continued to plummet with the 1953 strike over a contract dispute with ATU 192 that shut down transit services in the area for seventy-six days.[34] In 1955, the Transit District Law of the State of California adopted by the State Legislature provided the funding that enabled the creation of a special transit district owned by the public. Alameda and Contra Costa Counties citizens voted in 1956 to establish the Alameda–Contra Costa Transit District.

Once AC Transit was born in 1956, plans to provide adequate public transportation to East Bay residents were managed by the firm's board of directors, consisting of seven members elected by the voters to serve four year terms, from the start. The engineering firm De Leuw, Cather, & Company was hired in 1957 to provide the district with recommendations that it could use the transit facilities secured from Key System Transit Lines as well as the Greyhound Bus Lines operating within the district. Key System's operations at the time consisted of 321 buses for local service that operated out of three terminals, 142 buses for transbay service, and 47 multiple unit trains. AC Transit also acquired Key System's established 510 route miles for local service, 212 route miles for transbay bus lines, and 56 miles on the transbay rail lines.[35] While planners anticipated that the district would need route and service extensions, much of the board of directors' attempts to improve the quality of transit services that would be offered by AC Transit focused on shortening the trip time for patrons traveling among downtown districts of San Francisco, Oakland, and Berkeley.

The East Bay was not the only metropolitan area experiencing declines in public transportation. Between 1950 and 1960, the annual revenue from passenger fares on a national level, decreased from $13,845 million to $5,932 million, a 57 percent drop. Likely, the decline in ridership contributed to a continuing decline in employment at this time. As a result of this trend, the industry's total number of workers dropped from 240,000 in 1950 to 138,000 in 1970, a contraction of 42 percent. The transit industry's deteriorating financial health finally led to a shift from private to public ownership as private mass transportation companies could no longer continue to provide adequate bus services at affordable fares.[36]

As table 2.5 illustrates, between 1955 and 1969, cities with a population of less than 50,000 discontinued transit services, while cities with

Table 2.5 Changing status of transit companies by size of city and type of change, 1955–1969

Size of City	Becoming Public	Discontinuing Service	Total
Less than 25,000	6	51	57
25,000–50,000	15	40	55
Over 50,000	74	9	83
Total	95	100	195

Source: Darold T. Barnum, "From Private to Public: Labor Relations in Urban Transit," *Industrial and Labor Relations Review* 25, no. 1 (Oct. 1971): table 2, p. 99.

more than 50,000 people saw public transit authorities assume operation of their bus services. Congress passed legislation to support urban mass transit companies, ensuring that public transportation to urban areas did not disappear. Despite the growing number of public transit–reliant low-income families in urban areas, Congress passed the Urban Mass Transit Act of 1964 to support railroad companies threatening to discontinue the only commuter trains in America found in Chicago, New York, Boston, Philadelphia, and San Francisco. Urban planners and leaders contended that commuter trains were indispensable to the maintenance of employment opportunities in downtown areas.[37] The 1964 UMTA authorized the Department of Housing and Urban Development to provide grants to public agencies for purchasing vehicles and equipment in addition to improving facilities. Over time, the mission of UMTA has been extended to provide federal support to public transit agencies in every metropolitan area.[38]

Through UMTA and other policies, the transit public subsidy increased substantially from almost nothing in 1950 to an average of 60 percent of public subsidy from the 1960s through the 1980s. By 1980, operating assistance from the federal government had risen 17 percent higher than it had ever been, while state and local governments covered 40 percent of operating costs. At the same time, revenues from the fare box declined from 54 percent in 1975 to 37 percent just over a decade later in 1987.[39]

Despite declines in transit fare box revenue on the national level since the mid-1970s, AC Transit continued to expand its operations. By 1977, AC Transit's service area expanded to twenty-five cities and twelve major unincorporated areas within Alameda and Contra Costa Counties, providing transportation to one million people. During this time, AC

Transit offered a range of transit services to accommodate the patrons in this metropolitan area. Beyond providing East Bay local and transbay service, AC Transit began offering express bus service to BART stations in 1974 as well as services to the cities of Concord and Pleasant Hill in 1975, primarily to provide local transit services to BART customers in these cities who are commuting during the workday and shopping on Saturdays. AC Transit began providing services to the towns of Moraga and Orinda in 1976 and the cities of Antioch, Brentwood, and Pittsburg in 1977.[40]

While federal funds and local taxes certainly helped reinvigorate public transportation in the East Bay, efforts to go public were met with substantial opposition. In the case of Key System's transition to AC Transit, Robert Nisbet, a former AC Transit general manager, contends that antilabor and anti–public ownership sentiment caused most of the "feet-dragging" on this matter. Key System's corporate culture carried over to AC Transit because the same people who managed Key System managed the district. According to Nisbet, although many of these top managers were loyal to the district, others, such as Harold Davis, a former general manager who had been part of the "old gang," held stringent beliefs about labor relations and which traditions the transit system should uphold. For instance, before the transition to public, Key System did not hire women.[41]

While Key System had hired some White women during World War II when male workers were not available to do the job, the company stopped hiring them when the war ended. Like Davis, Alan L. Bingham, one of the first general managers of AC Transit, also had a problem with hiring women as transit operators, even after the firm began hiring more African American men as operators. Bingham kept the policy of barring women from employment intact by creating employment tests designed so that women would not generally pass them—test such as lifting fifty-pound weights. Nisbet, the firm's attorney, advised Bingham that these practices would not stand up legally; however, Bingham was stubborn about barring women from transit operator positions, making statements that women would be employed "over [his] dead body." AC Transit was not alone in their employment discrimination: South California Transit District and the Long Beach Transit District also took a position against hiring women as transit operators. As Nisbet recalls, "there was a common thinking among the transit operators that women just shouldn't be bus drivers."[42]

Due to these prejudices and other discriminatory employment patterns during the 1970s, AC Transit lost two class action lawsuits. In both cases, the court found that AC Transit discriminated against African American workers when it came to training for and promotion to positions within the firm. The Crutchfield v. Alameda–Contra Costa Transit District was filed on September 4, 1974, and the Pate et al. v. AC Transit case was filed in November 1975. In the first case, the plaintiffs were three African American women who attempted to secure positions as transit operators at AC Transit. Geraldine Crutchfield was eventually hired by AC Transit, and her coplaintiffs, Lucille Jackson and Peggy C. Parker had applied for jobs as transit operators at AC Transit but were refused employment. Crutchfield had first applied for a transit operator position at AC Transit in June 1970 and, despite her eight years of experience as a transit operator and her excellent driving record, was refused employment allegedly due to her inability to meet a 5'6" height requirement. Although she had certified proof from a doctor that her height was 5'6.5", AC Transit informed her that her poor driving record made her ineligible for consideration. Ms. Crutchfield decided to file a complaint with the Equal Employment Opportunity Commission and was eventually hired by AC Transit four years later in April 1974. After Ms. Crutchfield started work, however, she reported experiencing various acts of discrimination, including discrimination in training, discipline, and supervisor reports. In response, she filed an action against AC Transit once she received a "Notice of Right to Sue" from the U.S. Department of Justice.[43]

AC Transit refused plaintiff Lucille Jackson employment because she did not meet the company's height requirement. However, she joined this action because she felt that, despite the fact that she was 5'3" in height, she had the ability to perform all of the responsibilities associated with the job. She believed that the height requirement did not affect job performance and in turn decided to sue. The third plaintiff in this action, Peggy C. Parker, also applied unsuccessfully for employment with AC Transit in 1974. Despite her excellent driving record and her ability to meet the height requirement, she too alleged that she was denied employment, though in her case, the refusal was based on her failure to pass a written test.

The plaintiff class in this action contended that AC Transit's employment tests were not job-related and that the company was using them to screen out women applicants. Although AC Transit never admitted to any violation of Title VII of the 1964 Civil Rights Act or the equal protection secured by the Fourteenth Amendment, they settled the action with the plaintiffs and other members of the class the plaintiffs represented in May 1975, submitting a consent decree to the court as proof of their settlement of the dispute. In this decree, AC Transit agreed that "sex shall not be a consideration in recruitment and hiring . . . [and that] criteria relative to height, weight, color of eyes, color of hair, marital status, military status, credit status, arrest record, or information regarding spouses, family, friends, and hobbies [that] may have an adverse impact upon certain Title VII protected groups . . . shall [be] delete[d] from the application forms."[44]

As positions became available, AC promised to make every effort possible to hire more women transit operators as well as "to hire in accordance with the ethnic breakdown within each sex classification."[45] The court required AC Transit to make explicit in writing their hiring as well as employee evaluation procedures. Before 1975, AC Transit did not have any written hiring guidelines, including for clerical, maintenance, and management positions. Prior to that year, AC Transit's hiring practices typically involved showing preference to friends and relatives of current employees. In response to the court's requirement, AC Transit submitted samples of all tests used to hire and evaluate bus drivers and began drastically revising its hiring patterns.[46]

With the aid of a Berkeley consulting firm, AC Transit developed its first written Affirmative Action Plan on July 1, 1975, with which they claimed to "aggressively seek [the] advancement of groups which may have lagged behind in the work force." AC Transit hired John Rose, an African American male and East Bay Transit insider to serve as its first affirmative action coordinator. His job was to implement the plan and handle any discrimination complaints. As affirmative action coordinator, Rose sought employee opinion on the program's direction by establishing the Employee's Affirmative Action Advisory Committee April 24, 1975. AC Transit also demonstrated progress in its commitment to diversity through its annual cultural events, including Asian and Latin American celebrations, in addition to events occurring on Martin Luther King Jr. Day, Black History Month, and Women's History Month. What is more, AC Transit created jobs for employees with disabilities and founded diversity training programs for employees as a way to emphasize its commitment to all phases of diversity. The district also made efforts to feature diverse people in all advertisements.[47]

AC Transit's efforts to promote systemic change within the workplace generally centered on hiring and promotion efforts. To secure a diverse pool of applicants, the firm coupled shifts in its sorting and selection process with a broad advertising campaign in popular media targeting racial minorities. The firm also modified its promotion procedures, outlining promotion standards for each position and making efforts to alert all employees to available positions by posting notices on bulletin boards located in employee break rooms. While AC Transit introduced reforms, in the end, these actions did not improve the firm's culture of opportunity. In fact, as chapter 3 illuminates, when women—predominantly African American women—started entering the AC Transit workplace as transit operators in large numbers, their troubles were only just beginning.

3

Open Doors, Segregated Facilities

African American Women's Incorporation into AC Transit

Donna Pate entered AC Transit as a junior typist-clerk in the Transportation Department in March 1973. After promoting her to a full typist-clerk in July, the company transferred her to the Dial-A-Ride program. Pate later applied for a supervisory position in the Transportation Department's clerical unit but was denied the opportunity. J. Dale Goodman, the transportation manager, explained that he selected the White female candidate because of her secretarial experience. However, Pate felt certain that the woman, who had less experience and a shorter tenure with AC Transit than the African American women candidates for the position, had been selected on the grounds of her race: "She is White, and AC Transit management discriminates against minorities when they select employees for management and clerical positions."[1]

After unsuccessfully appealing to the Equal Employment Opportunity Commission (EEOC), Pate decided to pursue her case in court. She and the workers joining her in this 1975 class action lawsuit against AC Transit alleged that the company had violated Title VII by denying equal opportunities for training and promotion and by approaching disciplinary situations unfairly. Justice Orrick of the U.S. Court for the Northern District of California ruled that the hiring procedures in the company's clerical and maintenance units were not in fact discriminatory because seniority rules primarily governed access to these jobs. At the same time, the court did find that AC Transit discriminated against African American workers seeking promotion to supervisory and managerial jobs.[2]

In addition to the racial coding of applications, this class action lawsuit uncovered several exclusionary employment practices, including preferential hiring and subjective promotional standards. Before 1975, AC Transit did not have any written criteria for employment. By 1977, the informal policy of hiring friends and family of existing workers almost exclusively benefited White workers: the company frequently hired candidates recommended by White workers but regularly denied employment to candidates recommended by Black workers. That year, twenty-two pairs of related White employees worked at AC Transit, while the same year, there were only four pairs of related African American workers. Meanwhile, the clerical unit was actively coding applications by race in order to exclude African American women until late 1972 when the Urban Mass Transportation Administration objected to this practice. Once the government exposed these practices, the number of African American women employed in these positions increased substantially. In fact, 15 percent of new hires for clerical positions in 1973 were African American women.[3]

Evidence from the Pate et al. case further reveals that AC Transit did not promote African Americans to management positions outside of the Transportation Department between 1972 and 1977. Starting in 1975, AC Transit began using personnel analysts to screen for minimum qualifications and having the department supervisor interview each applicant. Nevertheless, when attempting to apply for a position outside of the Transportation Department, transit operators found themselves at a disadvantage because their seniority did not count outside of their department. For this reason, few African Americans—and especially few African American women—held managerial positions outside of the Transportation Department during this time. In fact, between 1975 and 1976, twelve out of the fifteen African American managers at AC Transit were in the Transportation Department. Most African Americans in managerial positions earned below the median wage of managerial workers in other AC Transit units.[4]

In 1979, the court in the Pate et al. case found the Consent Decree entered in 1975 too broad because it did not address opportunity hurdles in all major positions within the firm. Despite the decree, Judge Orrick note in the Opinion that AC Transit still neglected to develop written guidelines for hiring and continued to apply "purely subjective hiring standards by an exclusively white supervisory group." Since AC Transit could not counter the statistical evidence documenting its discriminatory hiring practices, the court found AC Transit liable to the plaintiff class for back pay due to discriminatory hiring and promotion practices used between 1972 and 1976. On June 19, 1981, the trial court additionally awarded the plaintiffs $147,040 in attorney's fees, though the U.S. Court of Appeals for the Ninth Circuit would reverse this decision in 1983.[5]

Unions have a history of claiming ignorance of discrimination allegations, despite the fact that many unions have a long track record of condoning job discrimination, and this was the case with the union representing the employees of AC Transit.[6] Because ATU 192's legal representation learned about the Pate et al. case after the court had found AC Transit guilty of discrimination, it decided not to intervene in the case. Peter Nusbaum, ATU 192's lead attorney, claimed there was no reason to intervene in the case since, in his view, the court was not likely to allow the union to intervene so late in the game. In a letter to Bill McCombe, president of ATU Local 192, Nusbaum wrote that the union's involvement was unnecessary because "the proposed consent decree actually gave the Black applicants less than what they might be entitled to." The consent decree only limited the rightful place seniority to only 15 individuals.[7]

African American employees were not the only people in the transit industry to suffer race-based discrimination; Latino American workers also suffered discrimination, as is clear in the case of Llamas et al. In this mid-1980s action, Latino American workers sued AC Transit for discrimination due to its failure to consider them for employment. Though AC Transit had adopted an Affirmative Action Plan as part of a consent decree in the Crutchfield v. AC Transit case and had in fact increased the number of African American transit workers, it had failed to increase the number of female transit operators and Latino American transit operators. What is more, between June 1976 and May 1978, AC Transit routinely hired far fewer Latino American transit operators than they had projected, and when it came to reporting the number of Latino Americans they had hired, they inflated the number by including individuals of Italian, Portuguese, Hawaiian descent—as well as other ethnic groups—in their calculations. At the conclusion of the case, plaintiffs Llamas, Aguirre, and Piccione received $2,500 each and company seniority payable upon the successful completion of their training.[8]

In the Llamas et al. case, ATU 192 alleged it had been unable to help determine whether AC Transit had discriminated in its recruitment, selection, and hiring procedures involving Latino American applicants. The union did not object to the fact that Latino Americans received retroactive "company seniority," which determines benefits not gained on a competitive basis. In correspondence with then ATU 192 president Al Johnson, the ATU attorney wrote that "AC Transit could make all the arguments relevant to the motion that the Union might have raised . . . and that [he] would also informally advise AC's attorney of [ATU's] position."[9]

While the Pate et al. and Llamas et al. cases exposed AC Transit's perpetual pattern of discriminatory hiring and workplace practices, evidence points to additional persistent interpersonal problems undermining AC Transit's capacity to provide a safe working environment to African American women transit workers, regardless of their position within the firm. In short, as this chapter shows, when AC Transit opened its door to previously excluded workers, placement decisions as well as the influence of gender and race antagonisms in the workplace compromised the company's ability to comply with recently established antidiscrimination laws and rulings.

Race- and Gender-Based Job Placements of Transit Operators

Following the Civil Rights Act and Affirmative Action regulations, AC Transit's hiring trends improved noticeably, especially with regard to the employment of women. However, while making efforts to employ women, by 1975, AC Transit developed a pattern of placing most African American women workers in a limited number of job categories within its divisions. Divisions are satellite facilities responsible for different routes within the service area, and each AC Transit worker is assigned to one of four divisions: Emeryville, East Oakland, Richmond, and Hayward/Newark. Here is where workers hang out, pick up their assignments, address most administration concerns, and drop off equipment at the end of the workday.

As table 3.1 illustrates, during 1972 and 1973, White men composed the majority of the incoming worker cohorts. By the time the company started hiring African American women as transit operators in 1974, the demographic makeup of the incoming workforce had changed significantly. By 1975, African American men composed the majority of incoming hiring cohorts, especially in the Emeryville (Division 2) and East Oakland (Division 4) Divisions. In 1977, AC Transit did not hire a single White male worker. Instead, regardless of division placement, the incoming hiring class that year consisted predominately of African American women.

During this time, African American women began to see large increases in their employment with AC Transit as operators, especially

Table 3.1 Percentage of transit operators in hiring class by race, gender, year, and division, 1972–1978

Year	Division	% White Male within Division	% Black Male within Division	% White Female within Division	% Black Female within Division
1972	Emeryville-D2	57	43	*	*
	Richmond-D3	74	26	*	*
	East Oakland-D4	78	22	*	*
	Newark-D6	*	*	*	*
1973	Emeryville-D2	64	36	*	*
	Richmond-D3	65	35	*	*
	East Oakland-D4	73	27	*	*
	Newark-D6	*	*	*	*
1974	Emeryville-D2	25	63	*	13
	Richmond-D3	59	41	*	0
	East Oakland-D4	54	44	*	2
	Newark-D6	*	*	*	*
1975	Emeryville-D2	15	35	10	40
	Richmond-D3	0	20	0	80
	East Oakland-D4	25	33	0	42
	Newark-D6	*	*	*	*
1976	Emeryville-D2	*	43	30	26
	Richmond-D3	33	17	17	33
	East Oakland-D4	20	53	4.1	22
	Newark-D6	100	*	*	*
1977	Emeryville-D2	*	8.5	40	51
	Richmond-D3	*	14	29	57
	East Oakland-D4	*	8.3	33	58
	Newark-D6	*	*	*	*
1978	Emeryville-D2	18	64	*	18
	Richmond-D3	0	83	*	17
	East Oakland-D4	22	56	*	22
	Newark-D6	*	*	*	*

N=643. * not in hiring cohort

Source: AC *Transit-Times* journals: 14, no. 7: 8–9; 14, no. 10: 8–9; 15, no. 1: 8–9; 13, no. 7: 8–9; 15, no. 4: 8–9; 15, no. 10: 8–9; 16, no. 1: 8–9; 16, no. 4: 8–10; 16, no. 7: 8–9; 16, no. 10: 10; 17, no. 1: 8–9; 17, no. 4: 8–9; 17, no. 7: 8–10; 17, no. 10: 8–9; 18, no. 1: 10; 18, no. 9: 8; 18, no. 10: 9; 19, no. 1: 8–9; 19, no. 4: 8–9; 19, no. 5: 10; 19, no. 8: 8–9; 19, no. 10: 8; 19, no. 11: 8; 19, no. 12: 8; 20, no. 3: 8–9; 20, no. 5: 9; 20, no. 8: 5; 20, no. 9: 9; 21, no. 5: 5; 21, no. 6: 9.

within the Richmond and East Oakland Divisions (Divisions 3 and 4, respectively). Newark is the only division that, between 1972 and 1978, did not place workers upon hire with the exception of one White man, who was placed at this division in 1976. Interviewees remarked that Newark/Hayward (Division 6) became a haven for higher seniority White male workers. According to many AC Transit operators, as the workforce within AC became predominately African American, especially within the Emeryville, East Oakland, and Richmond Divisions, some White male operators chose to separate themselves from African Americans by transferring to districts where fewer African American operators worked.

Differential Treatment Based on Sex: Problems with Coworkers and Passengers

Most of the transit operators I interviewed reported that when they started their jobs with AC Transit, they entered a hostile work environment where they often faced rude responses from both coworkers and patrons who did not appreciate an African American in their position. When African American women were first entering this occupation in the early to mid-1970s, many of the African American women transit operators who considered themselves "old-timers" mentioned that White men had a problem addressing African American women by their names. As one interviewee, Anne Marie recalls, "It was always 'gal' or 'girl,' and that was not acceptable." A few African American women interviewees even mentioned efforts by White men to intimidate them. Monica, the union steward, mentioned a situation where her male line instructor took them to Concord, pointing out where the Ku Klux Klan gathered and the pole they had used to hang people. Line instructors, Anne Marie explained, would try to plant the idea in the new hires' minds that, being women, they were not fit to work the job at hand. As Monica, the union representative, recalled, male coworkers would often say, "Go home. You know that you really can't handle this equipment. You need to speed up." Outside of the normal instruction that a line instructor would give a student if he were a male, Monica remembered comments like, "Well, you know you have children, and so you know that you won't be able to keep this job . . . [or they would say] this is a man's job. You're taking his job. Your husband should have this job. What kind of work does your husband do?" According to my interviews, the most direct and intense experiences of prejudice and harassment for African American transit operators, as was the case for Monica, occurred while training, regardless of an operator's tenure with the firm. Since the training period requires one-on-one interaction and is very short, most of the respondents mentioned that, while disturbing, the harassment during training did not upset them to the point of quitting their job.

Following their training, many operators reported intense exchanges with coworkers who vocally resisted the flood of women entering "their" work space and competing with them for "their" positions. This sentiment did not just come from White and Black male operators, but also from male patrons. As Ruth recalls, "I would have some men get on and say, 'You know you got my job don't you?' 'You know that you need to be at home taking care of your kids.'"

Given the findings regarding African American women's experience with sexual harassment in traditionally male-dominated workplaces such as firefighting, police work, and rail transit operation, it is not shocking to learn that the vast majority of African American women transit operators I interviewed either experienced some form of sexual harassment or knew someone who had to navigate this problem.[10] Some researchers contend that one function of sexual harassment is to drive women away from male-dominated workplaces. Others, such as Marian Swerdlow, maintain that harassment provides a way for men to welcome newly hired women workers but on interior terms. Based on her findings from a four-year participant observation study of African American women's incorporation into rail transit operative positions, Swerdlow concludes that "men as well as women developed accommodative practices when 'new women' arrived. Although the influx of female workers did not threaten these men's job security, it challenged their deeply held belief in male superiority by increasing the evidence that women could perform the same jobs competently. They responded not by attempting to oust women through harassment but by adapting collective interpretations of experience and practices that allowed them to preserve the ideology of male supremacy while accepting the entrance of women.[11]

Anita, a transit operator with seven years of experience at AC Transit, informed me that male coworkers treated women in her hiring class like "new booty." When I asked her how often men pressured women, she said, "it's like every morning. One guy cussed me out really bad because I would not talk to him. He went back and told his girlfriend that I was mad at him because he wouldn't give me any action. When she came to the job, I knew we had a problem. A fight happened, and AC Transit management investigated. He was suspended for a week and had to go to anger management."

Anita and her colleagues explained that male coworkers and supervisors measured their women colleagues' "womanhood" by their ability to tolerate sexual harassment. In fact, women transit workers reported that when they refused to give in to their male aggressors' advances, their femininity was challenged. Similar to the African American female police officers in Susan Martin's study, women transit operators who refused sexual advances were often accused of being "frigid," "a dyke," or invisible.

Sexual harassment at AC Transit was not only a problem, it was an intense and persistent problem. Similar to Mary Texeira's observations regarding sexual harassment in a U.S. law enforcement agency,[12] African American female transit operators at AC Transit reported that their African American male peers showered them with covert and persistent requests for dates and sex. According to transit operator interviewee, Sandra, "If you don't want to go on a date with them, and you are like, 'No, I'm fine, I got a man,' then they are like, 'You don't have to talk to me.' Or they try to belittle your self esteem. Some of the bold ones will not catch the hint. They come around every once in a while and say, 'I'm still waiting on your answer; when are we going to date?'"

A few women I interviewed suggested that some of these men were driven by more than attraction, by a sense of entitlement, their actions stemming from a notion that they had a right to pressure women at work for sex, despite their being married or in a relationship. As Tammy put it,

There are a lot of shifty men. I say this because they don't know how to talk to people, they say inappropriate things. They don't behave themselves, and they don't know how to take no for an answer. So, some of them are just trifling. They say and do stuff that they have no business doing, stuff that they would never say and do to another male operator unless they liked men. My thing is that we have got to start putting this stuff down on paper. These men who are not getting the play they want get upset whether you legitimately want men or not. They just do not like being turned down. So, some of them will disrespect you or treat you like you aren't a woman if you don't want them. The majority of them are married, and they introduce you to their wives. They are just trifling.

According to the transit workers I interviewed, inappropriate interest also came from male passengers, who sometimes voiced their opposition to women working "their" jobs. Ruth explained that this treatment occurred so frequently that workers became concerned about the boundaries between themselves and their patrons. When Ruth drove a bus, she said, "I had sexual attacks on me. Now, when I say sexual, I wasn't raped or anything. But, male passengers have tried to grab my breasts." Although Ruth was not sexually assaulted, at least one of her female colleagues reported "injury to nerves [due to] a sexual assault by [a] passenger at knifepoint," and many of other colleagues reported injuries resulting from the actions of irate male passengers, especially when driving Division 3 and 4 routes at night. A few years after AC Transit began hiring large numbers of African American women as transit operators, one Division 4 African American woman operator reported that a male passenger had hit her in the face with his fist as he left the bus, leaving her dazed with a swollen face, right ear pain, and a bruised lip. By 1980, several African American women transit operators had also found themselves rebounding from a punch to the face by a passenger. Among them, one African American woman transit operator reported being "hit twice in the face by [a] drinking passenger [who] . . . refused to pay [the] fare," while the same year another African American woman transit operator reported that she was assaulted by a passenger who was upset because he did not like where the bus stopped when it was time for him to exit. She was 3½ months pregnant at the time of the assault.[13]

In order to feel safe on the bus and in other environments where there was a potential for violence, African American women transit operators reported making use of various coping mechanisms. Ruth, whose bus route served some very rough neighborhoods, explained that, in order to be prepared, she came to work armed: "I brought my gun with me to work," she said. "I had children to go home to."

Responses to Sexual Harassment

While female African American transit operators needed to develop mechanisms to cope with potential violence by passengers, more immediate was the need to develop coping mechanisms for unwelcome attention by male coworkers and supervisors, which was rampant. Most of my interviewees explained that when it came to dealing with sexual harassment, they simply tried to ignore it. Operators Sandra and Mary did not let pressure from their patrons or colleagues bother them. As Sandra put it, "When somebody comes up behind me and says something, I just blow him off." Meanwhile, some women workers such as Ruth responded to sexual pressure vocally. As Ruth put it, "You know what, African American men and the white men treat us like pieces of meat . . . and some women do intermix with the guys, I mean management guys. But, I'm not going to get my rewards that way. I'm going to earn mine; I ain't laying on my back to get mine. That's why everything I have to say, I do not bite my tongue. I speak out. If I feel that you are violating me or anyone around me, I got your back. I do."

Another respondent decided to take her struggles with sexual harassment to federal mediators because AC Transit failed to address her concerns. Anna Marie explains:

> There was a lot of favoritism going on in terms of shifts, especially if you would not agree to date the supervisors coming after you. I had one instance where this person kept bothering me until he found somebody else to bother. Then, I guess in order to look good to her, he started giving her better shifts than me, even though I had the seniority. I complained about that. Then, he started to exploit things, like looking at little things that he thought could show that I'm doing wrong. He also would scream and cuss at me. So, I went through the chain of command and nothing happened. Then I went downtown to the EEOC and they came down and investigated. All this quieted down after that. He was given a set of instructions regarding this situation that he followed.

Patti Giuffre and Christine Williams have found that while some women may be vocal and aggressive in their efforts to avoid sexual harassment, most women are unlikely to devote much energy to fighting this form of on-the-job abuse because they view their discomfort around sexually aggressive male coworkers as "something you just put up with" to keep your job. Giuffre and Williams also suggest that some women who experience sexual harassment on the job are not aware that it is illegal, while others repress their concerns because they fear no one will believe them.[14]

Over the years, many women transit operators began voicing their concerns about harassment by suing AC Transit. Yolanda Jones, an AC Transit operator filed a case with the U.S. District Court in May 2000, claiming that AC Transit failed to protect her from harassment when she encountered threatening behavior by Edras Gonzales, a fellow AC Transit operator. Jones claimed that Gonzales caused her to become immediately concerned for her health and safety when both buses stopped at the corner of 40th Street and Broadway in the city of Oakland. According to Jones, Gonzales was "upset, exited his bus, and approached [Ms. Jones], while leveling a barrage of profanity." As a consequence of this verbal attack, Jones returned to the bus yard and reported the concerns to Acting Superintendent Bob Estrella, who encouraged her to submit a written account of Gonzales's actions. Despite the urging to report this event, Jones never received a follow-up from her supervisors. Jones further stipulates that on or about December 3, 1999, Gonzales involved another male driver in their drama by encouraging this driver, German Zambrano, to make choking and throat-cutting gestures at Jones, while Gonzalez rode as a passenger on Zambrano's bus. The last event occurred on or about December 9, 1999, when Gonzales approached Jones and tried to engage her in discussion. When she chose not to entertain him, Gonzales called her "a bitch" and other obscenities that caused her to fear for her safety. She then called the police for backup since AC Transit had demonstrated their inability to protect her from Gonzales's behavior.[15]

Once the officers arrived, they contacted Jones's supervisors and requested that she be relieved from duty because they feared that her poor mental state would have an adverse effect on her driving abilities. Throughout this time, Jones claimed that she was under medical care for headaches and stress related to AC Transit's inability to protect her from harassment and discrimination on the job. A mediation was scheduled for December 10 at which she and Gonzales were to attempt to resolve the matter, but the session was postponed until December 16 because the conflict resolution program director was unavailable. After receiving news of the postponement, Jones did not return to work on December 13 and 14 due to her fear of continued harassment by Gonzales. Because Jones failed to report to work on these days, AC Transit terminated her employment. She filed a complaint with the EEOC for wrongful termination, claiming that AC Transit fired her in retaliation for her complaints of unlawful harassment as well as because of AC Transit's "desire to protect its male employees and predominately male workforce."[16] When she later elected to pursue the case in state court, this claim was dismissed.

Other employees, including Rosemary James, also decided to sue AC Transit for allowing sex-based differential treatment to occur without instituting corrective measures to address the offenses. Starting in October 1988, James worked for AC Transit as the Compensation and Benefits Administrator. In this position, the company treated James as a bona fide executive exempt from overtime provisions of the Fair Labor Standards Act (FLSA).[17]

James underwent surgery on December 8, 1989, to address ongoing reproductive health concerns and was scheduled to be absent from work for six weeks during her recovery. After consulting with her doctor in early January 1990, however, James learned that she could return to work on a limited basis. When James shared this news with her supervisor, Dorothy Parrish, her supervisor suggested that she return to work on a part-time basis and, under FLSA, recommended that she be compensated as though she were working full time. Parrish supported her recommendation by noting that James was a dedicated AC Transit employee who worked "in excess of eight hours per day." However, when Chuck Hill, the assistant to the general manager learned on January 10 that James would return on a part-time basis and receive her full salary, he instructed her to return home until the district decided whether it would pay her full salary while she worked on a part-time basis.[18]

On January 17, AC Transit decided not to let James work part time and receive her full salary. The district also denied her request for retroactive compensatory time to make up for the hours she could not work, though AC Transit did allow her to use her sick leave to cover the gap in pay between January 17 and January 31. On January 28, James filed a grievance claiming that AC Transit was not at liberty to reduce her pay for absences less than a full day because she was an exempt employee under the FLSA. The district did not respond to this complaint until March 6, 1991, wherein Assistant to the General Manager Michal Settles communicated that the district would not approve the excused leave with pay.

In her complaint, James stated that, because she routinely observed other managers receiving accommodations for time missed, she believed AC Transit had handled her situation inequitably. In fact, she recalled instances where the district approved full pay for part-time work by employees who did not suffer reproductive system illnesses or health conditions. She noted that these partial day absences were not reported to the Payroll Department and that AC Transit allowed some employees to make up time rather than have their pay docked.[19]

James based her contention that AC Transit was treating her differently because of her sex as well as her observation that the company tended to favor departments primarily employing men. She explained, "Employees in the human resources department (which has a female manager and is comprised of mostly female employees) are consistently treated differently by Mr. Hill than employees in his other departments (all of which are headed by male employees)." James added that "Mr. Hill has personally instructed me and other employees to grant favors to various male employees which conflicted with District policy, moral and ethical considerations, [in addition to] sound human resources practices and the law." In cases involving male employees, James claimed that Mr. Hill "has either overridden the policy or practice or has aggressively sought and secured approval of the General Manager and the Board of Directors."[20]

In the end, James requested compensation for the days AC Transit required her to stay home, approval of excused leave with pay, and the addition of forty-eight hours to her sick leave balance for the half days of sick leave she was required to use. While the district decided to pay her for the days the company had required her to stay at home, AC Transit denied both her request for excused leave with pay and her request for the reinstatement of her sick leave. In response to their decision, James filed a complaint on July 17, 1991, for violation of the FLSA. This lawsuit was later dismissed with prejudice pursuant to an undisclosed settlement agreement and general release of all claims executed between the parties on August 31, 1993.[21]

During this time, Dorothy Parrish, a labor relations manager for AC Transit, filed an EEOC complaint claiming that, in violation of Title VII of the Civil Rights Act of 1964, AC Transit failed to promote her to a vacant assistant general manager position in October 1989. She mentioned in her complaint that "the individual hired was a male who was less qualified," and she contended that the general manager, who ultimately held the hiring authority and who "indicated through other actions and statements his unwillingness to treat women equitably [in] employment matters" did not grant her an interview. Parrish initiated the complaint process in November 1989 soon after learning that the company was denying her promotion to the position of human resource manager. Instead, the company hired a White male, who, she claimed, had no managerial experience, while she had experience as a human resources manager.[22]

In her EEOC complaint, Parrish contended that the general manager for administration often referred to women as "girls" and "baby" in addition to portraying women in a disparaging light. In its determination letter, the EEOC claimed it did not find evidence to substantiate Parrish's allegation that AC Transit created an environment hostile to the female sex. The EEOC did establish that the director of transportation often referred to women (and men) as "baby" and that he was aware that several women employees considered this term offensive. When the EEOC learned about his language, it required the director of transportation to receive counseling regarding sexual harassment and to view a video on the subject called *All the Wrong Moves*. Although the EEOC's investigation did not find evidence AC Transit had discriminated against Parrish when she applied for the positions of assistant general manager for administration and labor relations manager, she did receive the right to pursue her claims in federal district court.

In the federal complaint Parrish filed in the U.S. District Court, Northern District of California, she added a further allegation, claiming that AC Transit failed to promote her in 1989 because of actions she took as the human resources manager, namely her expression of concerns about the company's hiring decisions that were inconsistent with the district's Affirmative Action/Equal Employment Opportunity plan and compliance requirements. Parish claimed that, as a result of discrimination and an as an act of retaliation, she received unequal treatment from AC Transit relative to the treatment of similarly situated male workers in terms of pay increases, promotional opportunities, and grievance resolutions as well as additional terms and conditions of employment.[23]

Because AC Transit and Parrish reached a settlement in 1993, Parrish's case against AC Transit was dismissed with prejudice. According to this "Employment and Consulting Agreement," AC Transit hired Parrish to work on special projects using her expertise and knowledge of human resources. According to the agreement, she would begin this work after resigning from her position as human resources manager. In addition to transferring her position from manager of human resources to manager of special projects, the contract specified that she would receive the same salary and benefits. While her employment with AC Transit ended May 1, 1994, AC Transit kept her on as a consultant between May 2, 1994, and November 23, 1994, agreeing to pay Parrish, who represented herself in these proceedings, $36 per hour and a $12,000 settlement. In return, AC Transit never offered an admission of liability, and Parrish agreed to drop her lawsuit and agreed never again to apply for an AC Transit position. Lastly, she agreed not to share "confidential and proprietary information concerning AC Transit's employment and personnel practices" unless pursuant to subpoena.[24]

Differential Treatment on the Job Based on Race: Problems with Passengers and Coworkers

Many transit operators I interviewed experienced fear at the start of their AC Transit careers because they were assigned the least desirable runs and had to serve the poorest and most dangerous communities in the district. Some suffered daily run-ins with rude and boisterous youth, and others had to learn to manage the unpredictable behavior of riders on drugs and other substances. Transit operators also mentioned that they had to contend with harassment by patrons whose behavior appeared to be racially motivated. Ruth, who has been employed by AC Transit since 1975, said that many people call the drivers derogatory names. As she recalled, "I have been called a nigger plenty of times. I had a little White woman get on the 40 bus and say that she'll beat me like I was a slave." Ruth responded, "I will beat your ass with your own umbrella, okay!" This is just one of many such incidents. "One time," Ruth recalled, "I was driving the school in Berkeley on the West campus, and a little girl got on the bus. Little fast heffer, White. She spit on me and I beat her ass. I told her I'm about to do what your mother and father wouldn't do. They tried to make me apologize. They brought charges up on me and everything. But, I would not apologize. I thought what you need to do is teach her to keep her spit to herself."

Once job conditions improved for transit operators and their wages became public information, drivers began encountering riders who seemed overly critical and demeaning due to their assumption that African Americans are not fit to perform the job. Later, it became known that a high-ranking employee of AC Transit had been encouraging this assumption. In fact, AC Transit was eventually forced to suspend an official over racially biased and sexist remarks he made in 1990 at an affirmative action meeting welcoming a sixteen-member group of transit officials. The union members present at this event claimed that the then top AC Transit official Robert H. Garside, who had just been hired by the company earlier that year to oversee fleet maintenance, blamed the district's service problems on the hiring of "inept women and minorities" and his contention that the "union was running the district." According to Ely Hill, ATU 192 president, Garside claimed that the district's

Affirmative Action program did not properly screen for skill, which "forced him to hire minorities and women." AC Transit publicly stated that the union's version of events was untrue and designed to stir up problems.[25]

Contrary to AC Transit's contentions about Garside's comments, three people who attended the meeting reported to the *Tribune* that Garside did in fact assert that AC Transit's Affirmative Action programs caused them to select unqualified workers but claimed Garside did not refer to these workers as "inept." While each of these three was a member of various racial groups and two were women, all reported to the *Tribune* that they did not take offense at Garside's comments. At the same time, one of these attendees, supervising engineer at the State Department of Transportation Cindy Quon recalled that one of the attendees felt the need to ask Garside during a break whether he had concerns with the work of minorities. Quon reported that Garside answered "No" and that he seemed to her to be primarily concerned about employing qualified workers.

Although the general manager at the time, Tim O'Sullivan, told the AC Transit board that Garside's comments were not as "inflammatory" as the union claimed, O'Sullivan nevertheless took measures to quell any flames. He issued a written apology to the sixteen individuals who had attended the meeting of the Bay Area Urban Transit Institute where Garside expressed his opinion about AC Transit's Affirmative Action program. O'Sullivan also decided to suspend Garside for one week and, for the purposes of addressing long-standing complaints regarding discrimination, announced that he would begin sensitivity training at AC Transit and hire an independent investigation to examine affirmative action complaints. Meanwhile, union officials, including Ed Jackson, Local 192 business agent, continued to support Garside's firing. Claiming that O'Sullivan's response to the matter was just "window dressing," Jackson stated that "anything less [than firing Garside] would send out the message that the East Bay and AC Transit think it is OK for our public officials to be racist, sexist, and antiunion." After his one-week suspension, Garside worked for AC Transit for an additional six years before becoming Houston's metro assistant general manager for maintenance.

Regardless of Garside's intent, his statements provoked a great deal of criticism in the larger community, and it prompted the union to threaten a wildcat strike if AC Transit failed to fire him. Garside's comments not only offended the drivers but met with criticism on the part of other workers employed by AC Transit as well. One Maintenance Department clerk remarked that many of her women and minority colleagues were "appalled" by the statements. She added, "I know that kind of feeling existed, but [I did not know that] nobody was stupid enough to say it."[26]

Responses to Race Discrimination

African American transit operators employed by AC Transit used a variety of coping strategies when it came to facing race-based discrimination by the firm as well as by passengers. Some transit operators chose to sue or challenge the district's decision to punish them for having to protect them from the racist and sexist coworkers and patrons as well as other oppressive conditions. Thomas Dycus, an AC Transit operator hired in 1981, sued the district for wrongful termination based on a provoked altercation with an irate driver. Dycus, who held an excellent service record and was the recipient of various safety awards, suffered an attack by an angry driver on October 25, 1988. While in the "ducking and blocking punches and kicks," Dycus knocked his attacker to the ground.[27]

Dycus provided a written account of the incident to his superiors shortly after the incident, but nonetheless, on December 1, 1988, AC Transit found him guilty of preventable criminal behavior and gross misconduct involving rudeness, abusive behavior, and neglecting his duties as a driver to engage in a physical altercation. Following his unsuccessful arbitration hearing in April 1989, Dycus filed a lawsuit against AC Transit, claiming that he did not deserve to be terminated for this incident. He claimed that AC Transit did not give him an opportunity to challenge the claims voiced by his accuser at his arbitration hearing and that the company failed to let him to voice his side of the story. Dycus further argued that the company had no right to fire him when it did not fire White transit operators who had suffered similar conflicts and only disciplined them for their role in the altercations. Ely Hill, the president of ATU, Local 192, wrote a one-sentence statement in support of Dycus's claim, stating his awareness of other cases "where other drivers fought with passengers in the public and were not discharged."[28]

Dycus additionally contended that AC Transit failed to take into account other mitigating factors, namely his fear for his well-being while on the job. Just ninety days prior, one of Dycus's best friends, Billy Joe Givens, had been fatally shot by a passenger for no cause while working as a transit operator on the same bus line Dycus was driving the night of the altercation. In addition to this tragic loss, Dycus had had an altercation with a group of youth prior to the altercation for which he was being terminated. According to his Oakland Police Department report, one of the kids in the group had pointed a gun at Dycus, and Dycus, along with another of the youth, had to convince the kid not to shoot. Not more than thirty minutes later, Thomas was in a near collision with the irate driver of the car who hit and kicked him. Thomas argued in this complaint that AC Transit failed to consider its responsibility to develop safe working conditions, and that its failure to devise a safety plan encouraged the public to disrespect and attack bus drivers. Ultimately, Dycus's claim against AC Transit was dismissed in January 1992.[29] This was not only an unfortunate outcome for Dycus, but also for others in the community who appreciated his commitment to his job. Ida Tielenburg of San Leandro, California, wrote a complimentary note that was published in AC Transit's publication *Transit Times*. In this note, she called Dycus "a good professional driver—one who thinks quickly where there is a danger."[30]

Like Dycus, transit operator Leonard Leroy resisted what he believed to be unfair treatment by AC Transit following a physical altercation in which he found it necessary to remove an argumentative passenger from the bus. He received a twenty-one-day suspension, which he appealed. Leroy's incident with the passenger occurred just after the passenger missed the bus. The passenger drove to another stop to get on the coach and began to ask Leroy repetitively why he did not wait for him. This inquiring did not end until Leroy removed the passenger from the bus in the front of two supervisors. Despite the fact that Leroy and the passenger had been experiencing ongoing friction, Leroy failed to win this arbitration because he could not prove that the passenger provoked him. In the end, Leroy could not prove his claim that the passenger was racist because he did not have any proof to support this conviction.[31]

Leroy maintained that his experience was a case of covert racism. As he put it, "the majority of the passengers on my coach were white, and I'm, in certain cases, I'm the only Black person on board." Leroy explained that "by his behavior, I felt that he was trying to be an opportunist in that moment. 'Let me just embarrass this Black person in front of all these White folks on the coach.'" Traditionally, covert racism is very difficult to prove, and Leroy's case was no exception.[32]

Based on the number of lawsuits filed against AC Transit, transit operators were not alone in voicing concerns about covert discrimination.

Other workers of color employed by AC Transit reported similar workplace concerns. On January 28, 2004, AC Transit notified Rozella Johnson of her impending termination from her position as an executive secretary for AC Transit Manager Kathleen Kelly. In her claim, Johnson explained that she had received a letter from the hearing officer notifying her that she had five business days to appeal the termination. The sudden termination seemed incongruent with feedback Johnson had received from previous managers she had worked for in the company. Prior to Kelly, Johnson had reported to three high-level mangers over the course of her eighteen years with AC Transit, and each of the managers had commended her job performance. Moreover, while the district claimed she had not taken any courses to improve her computer skills, Johnson presented the hearing officer copies of certificates demonstrating her completion of various software courses taken while she was reporting to Kelly.[33] Johnson testified that throughout their working relationship, Kelly had treated her in a "condescending, belittling and demeaning manner," beginning with requests for her to remove ripped up paper and debris from Kelly's desk, a task that Kelly did not ask Caucasian employees to perform. Due to Kelly's treatment of Johnson as well as Kelly's habit of making comments insinuating that Johnson did not arrive at her job motivated to work, Johnson filed an EEOC complaint in 1997.

Johnson was not the only African American employee at AC Transit to suffer discrimination under Kelly. Francois Njike, the only other African American in their department reporting to Kelly, filed a verified complaint claiming that Kelly instigated his termination from AC Transit in 2000 and that his termination demonstrated a pattern of discriminatory treatment of African Americans working under Kelly. According to Njike, Kelly did not treat her Caucasian subordinates in the way she treated the African American workers who answered to her; in fact, he recalled that she persistently harassed him both at work and at home. In his deposition, Njike reported that she would yell and scream at him and that she failed to alter her negative appraisals of his job performance. He also recalled that she would call him at home at one o'clock in the morning, "telling me how I messed up the bus stop, yelling and screaming." He said that this treatment continued until he was terminated from AC Transit.[34]

In Njike's deposition for the Johnson case, he could not recall specific instances of race discrimination toward Johnson, but he did recall

Kelly yelling and screaming at Johnson. In his deposition, Njike noted that "she'll [Kathleen Kelly] pass by, walk into her office, and come out and call Rozella in, and I would hear the way she would give her orders through the door from the office. Kathleen might call her into her office and talk to her in a way that I was like, 'Whoa.' This is a slave owner talking to the workers, like a farmworker; that's what it was like."[35]

On October 6, 1991, Johnson filed a formal complaint in response to Kelly's work appraisal, claiming that Kelly's wrongful treatment of her stemmed from a racial bias against her and that this treatment resulted in Johnson suffering mental health issues requiring her to take antidepressant medication. Other high-level managers at AC Transit, including former General Manager Sharon Banks, an African American, questioned whether it was Johnson's job to "fetch personal things for Ms. Kelly during meeting." Former AC Transit employee Candy Williams-Scarlett also observed Kelly's harassment of African Americans, but because she was unwilling to involve herself in the case while employed at AC Transit due to fear of retaliation, her observations did not play a part in the hearing.[36]

Based on the precedent of the Ninth Circuit Court of Appeals in Schneider v. San Diego County (9th Circuit 2001) 24 Fed. App. 744, which recognized the right of a public employee to request reassignment to a nonharassing supervisor, Johnson argued that she had a right to be reassigned. In Schneider v. San Diego County, the Court of Appeal found that the plaintiff, who claimed permanent incapacity for disabling purposes, should have been allowed to return to work in a different position where he would be safe from any harassment or retaliation. Like this plaintiff, Johnson claimed that the company should have offered her the opportunity to work for a supervisor other than Kelly because her psychiatric disability had directly resulted from a work environment tainted by Kelly's harassment and retaliation. Johnson further contended that her inability to focus and concentrate on her duties at work due to her work environment had led to her termination, and she asked the court to determine whether AC Transit had an obligation to accommodate her disclosed mental disability.

In the end, the judge did not rule in favor of Johnson. First, he found Johnson unable to establish pretext. Though the general manager had testified in his deposition that he was aware of Johnson's discrimination complaints prior to her termination, Johnson, according to the judge, did not exercise reasonable diligence in presenting this testimony at her hearing. Moreover, the judge argued that Johnson failed to offer a theory as to why Kelly treated her harshly. The judge maintained that the case was weak because Johnson's claim relied primarily on the testimony of just two people: Njike and Johnson. Additionally, the judge asserted that Johnson failed to identify other employees outside of her protected class being treated inequitably under similar circumstances. Johnson was eventually approved for vested retirement from AC Transit, effective starting October 1, 2006. AC Transit Board minutes dated January 23, 2008, note that board members voted to "authorize the waiver of costs in exchange for not filing an appeal by the Plaintiff."[37] In short, Johnson agreed not to file an appeal, and AC Transit covered the costs of the litigation.

Summary

Just as workplaces and mobility opportunities are not "gender neutral," neither are these social spaces racially neutral.[38] Workplaces are gendered in terms of work placements and social divisions,[39] while also being structured by racial stereotypes and divisions that shape patterns of interaction and occupational returns.[40] In this chapter, I illustrated intersections between race and gender divisions and documented how these intersections affected the workplace experiences of African American women transit operators and other similarly situated workers employed by AC Transit.

Building on Patricia Hill Collins's concept "outsiders within," my analysis of African American women in White male–dominated professions focused on how they gained access to these jobs and the degree to which they experienced marginalization on the job, especially in terms of placement and promotions. On the whole, most African American female transit operators reported that ongoing racial prejudice and sexual harassment played a role in shaping their ability to move up the ladder. However, since the racial stereotypes African American women transit operators encounter make them vulnerable to similar hardships facing African American men in the labor market, transit operators such as Anne Marie maintain that racial membership ultimately limits career trajectory within AC Transit. As Anne Marie mentioned,

[We have to look at] what kind of job do they have? What position are they holding? That is what needs to be looked at, and when you talk about being promoted, in what areas are we being promoted? And if not, why not? I don't think that this is a race issue because of what I'm lacking, or [because] I don't want to look at myself and do what I need to do. I see this as a race issue because I'm just as qualified and experienced as the other person that got the job, and I didn't.

Monica backs up Anne Marie's statement regarding the difficulty of African American women moving into district-level management. As she put it, "as far as promotions into district level management, where you move away from driving, it doesn't seem to be a lot of discrimination at that level. But, when you start to go beyond that level, that's when you see that it is discrimination against Black men, Latinos, it doesn't matter. It's all about the White face . . . as you go up the ladder and you move from the divisional levels, you're working downtown at 1600 Franklin. That's where you see a remarkable difference."

While racial and gender antagonisms have continued to undermine the structure of opportunity available to African American women workers, the transit operators I interviewed reported that they were able to adjust to race and sex antagonisms because they needed their jobs and were willing to tolerate the disagreeable and inequitable conditions that came with them. Other workers could not maintain or upgrade their position within the urban transit workplace because the glass ceiling—and in some cases harassment and violence—proved too difficult to overcome. But a racial and gendered workplace was not the only challenge African American women transit workers faced. As they secured more jobs in the industry, they also found themselves shouldering significant work/life imbalances and facing numerous workplace hazards—as chapter 4 explores.

4

A Rough Ride

How Worker-Centered Reforms, Ambivalence, and
Declining Conditions Create Work/Life Conflicts

We come to work here, this is our livelihood, but there are certain
things that are over and above. [For instance] if my child is home sick
and I call in and say, "I can't come in because my child is sick," and
you tell me, "Well, my manpower doesn't allow me to excuse you,"
well, you do what you have to do because I'm going to be here with
my child . . . managers are not sensitive to the needs of human beings.
We're not machines.

—Wayne, ATU 192 Union Officer, 1990

Wayne, a union officer spoke with passion throughout a 1990 interview
exploring the factors that contributed to absenteeism within AC Transit. In a position that he shared with ATU 192 President Ely Hill, this
officer argued that "managers slide by the issues simply with discipline. . . .
They don't want to be sensitive to people and sit down and try to ratio-
nalize with those employees about the situation of attendance." These
union leaders argue that "everybody's priorities are in the wrong place
because more emphasis is placed on assigning blame than showing com-
passion or a willingness to understand how the pressures in their lives
conflict with their capacity to commit to the job."[1]

Many of the African American women initially hired as transit operators by AC Transit were single mothers. Due to the stress of the job
and their ability to secure child care for their children, a substantial share
of the women hired in the late 1970s and 1980s could not hold onto the
job because working late hours and long shifts interfered with their capacity to parent.[2] Beyond the work/life imbalances and industrial injuries, most of absent workers who were not sick increasingly began to
avoid work because the working conditions became extremely stressful.
As Wayne, the union officer notes, "you get up in the morning, you feel
fine, you go to work, everything's nice—the first one gets on the bus wants
to call you a son of a bitch. No reason at all, because something happened

with him. . . . You try to let that pass by, but the next one gets on, he's going to call you something else."[3]

I imagine that these kinds of circumstances, possibly combined with bad weather, congested Bay Area traffic, and a full bladder are not anyone's idea of a great start to the day. But, this has been the daily reality of many transit operators employed by AC Transit, especially since the early 1980s. Although AC Transit employs four assistant superintendents, one at each division, whose job primarily consists of dealing with absenteeism and handing out discipline, ATU 192 maintained in their 1990 interview that there's "nobody there to deal with the problems that the employees themselves are having." The contract allows management to engage work and life imbalances through informal reviews. However, union officers interviewed in 1990 reported that AC Transit elected to implement attendance policies that treated all worker absences as identical, whether they were absent due to a late night out or because of a legitimate medical excuse.[4]

AC Transit management saw things very differently. This transit district contended that it was doing its best to offer accessible and cost-effective services to Bay Area patrons who still depended on the mass transit firm. Because federal funding was decreasing and the firm was in fierce competition with BART for local transit dollars, AC Transit's upper level management considered itself a sinking ship that required desperate action to save. Despite massive deficits and high rates of turnover among high-level managers, AC Transit continued to advocate for funding and promote its ability to provide high-quality transit services. However, while emphasizing funding constraints, the transit company thought that it was appropriate to place the blame for the service complaints primarily on the workers operating the buses. A needs assessment by the consultancy Booz, Allen, and Hamilton suggested to the AC Transit management that absent workers were contributing to rising labor costs as a result of sick leave pay, coverage staff compensation, and the administrative costs associated with recruiting hiring and training workers. In response, the firm decided to implement an absenteeism policy that disciplined workers for excessive absences for "whatever his or her reason."[5]

Compared to twenty transit properties in 1989, AC Transit ranked the worst with an absentee rate of 18 percent and the peer average was 8 percent.[6] In turn, despite the fact that within the company 85 percent of all absences were due to sick leave and industrial injury and another 8 percent were excused absences,[7] AC Transit was persistent in its attempts to implement attendance control policies that especially targeted transit operators and maintenance workers as opposed to the firm's other clerical and managerial employees. According to opinions voiced by AC Transit managers, there was something different about the latest cohorts of transit workers employed by the district. In the district's opinion, the transit operators who had been hired as a result of antidiscrimination laws and legal pressures were not as committed to the job as previous workers and efforts to address the problems of absenteeism with programs such as flex-time programs were overrated. Although the company made efforts to boost morale by offering coffee and donuts and making fruit available to workers in break rooms, these efforts were expensive and short-lived in the face of high absenteeism. So, when all else failed, AC Transit made efforts to rid itself of these workers who didn't come to work "regardless of reasons or establishment of fault" and has maintained a version of policy ever since.[8]

When thinking about the major factors contributing to issues like absenteeism, it is easy to place the onus on the individual whose actions signify a disinterest in maintaining his or her employment. Every workplace has employees who (for whatever reasons) don't show up on time and/or consistently or who lack a real commitment to the job itself. But the evidence from my research suggests that this has not been the practice among operators at AC Transit. Evidence suggests that the transit operators were frequently making secondary adjustments within this environment that has been increasingly encroaching on their personal lives. Stress steadily increased among transit operators due to the changing run schedules, constant turnover, and daily risks of contending with the East Bay traffic and issues of race and gender inequality within AC Transit. It was not surprising to find within union records evidence suggesting that many of these workers were burnt out and using absenteeism to contend with their discontent, mental strain, and unaddressed work/life conflicts. This chapter explores what ATU 192 and AC Transit chose to do about absenteeism as well as about the work/life imbalances and shifts in the job quality that contributed to this problem. I also explore how these organizations' responses to productivity concerns shaped the structure of opportunity available to African American women and similarly situated workers.

On the Realities of Work as an African American Woman Transit Operator

"Sacramento, University," Frances called out to her passengers. Then, after making a few more stops and navigating through busy traffic, she turned to me and said, "now, don't say nothing about me talking on the phone because that could cause a problem." This Oakland native, never-married single mother of a twelve-year-old son did not have time to get caught breaking one of the company's rules. With no help at home from her son's father and limited assistance from family and friends, she had to raise her preteen the best way she could while working her "40 plus" hour schedule with AC Transit, which averaged to about sixty-five hours per week, including overtime. Like many of the transit operators I interviewed, Frances depended on this job because, as she recalled, "I was getting an income that was more than I had been getting before; [plus] I could take care of my son properly."

But it turns out that keeping the job while managing one's responsibilities as a single parent has been a very difficult task, even for someone like Frances who was "super excited" to land an operator position with AC Transit seven years ago. Frances described her initial part-time placement as "horrible" because it was a night shift that guaranteed interactions with "your riffraff, the people that have nothing to do, but come out and hassle other people." To make matters worse, she did not have her own transportation to work. When she first started the job, she would have to take her son to the babysitter at 3 A.M. in the morning. Then, hop on the BART and travel to a stop where she could afford a taxi ride to the Hayward Division Training Center. Frances wanted and needed the job so badly that she drove the 82-Owl for two years before transferring to a better shift and route in the Richmond Division.

Even though "it's a lot of rules for a bus driver," Frances tries to "keep it clean" by "going to work, getting there on time, and hoping that [she will] leave on time." Frances mentioned that most of her problems at work have been due to absences caused by her inability to find a place for her son when he was sick. Lately, her problem has been using a cell phone while on duty. Although she said that "you can lose your job over talking on the phone while you're driving," Frances also acknowledged that using phones while driving has been a big problem because "most of us have children . . . and if you see your kid's number pop up on your phone, naturally you want to answer it. But, you aren't supposed to unless it is an emergency." Workers like Frances often times jeopardize their ability to keep their job by missing work as well as occasionally making and receiving phone calls to find out their kids' whereabouts.

Research from other studies on transit work suggests that work/life conflicts are common among most transit operators. As an Asian father in Blanche Grosswald's study said, "I Raised My Kids on the Bus," which came with some regrets, as he puts it, "my biggest concern was that I felt like I wasn't as close to my kids as I should have been. And I think that had a lot to do with the hours I was working." According to an African American mother in Grosswald's study, when you are working as a transit operator "you really have no family life. We are here so much that there are people whose children are born, go to school, and get married and they've never attended any of the family events. They've never been to their high school graduations because they couldn't get time off. The job is not setup to allow for family life."[9]

AC Transit operators who did not cite child care responsibilities as their Achilles' heel on the job mentioned that their quality of health impacted their ability to keep the job. Before securing a dispatcher position, Ruth, who has over twenty-five years of experience as a driver, mentioned that a nagging back injury kept her from driving and that she almost lost her job because she could not drive due to intense pain. Transit workers like Mary, who has worked for AC Transit for five years, contend that the work equipment wreaks havoc on their health and well-being. As Mary put it, "the seats are all jacked up. All of us will eventually have back problems, shoulder problems and knee problems in our older years . . . because of the seats and the way they bounce. Sometimes when I get home I may have daggers shooting up my back. Then, I go to the doctor and they give me physical therapy when it gets bad."

Mary is not the first transit operator to cite issues with equipment that causes pain on and off the job. In fact, it turns out that AC Transit has a long history of entertaining the concerns of injured workers. Beyond the health concerns and job loss caused by equipment on the bus, transit operators mentioned that one of the chief factors driving AC Transit's missed runs, incidents, and high rates of absenteeism, which occurred with alarming regularity throughout the 1980s, was the general condition of the district's buses. Although AC Transit's maintenance operations were commended throughout the 1960s and the early 1980s, by the end of the 1980s, the *Tribune* joined other Bay Area newspapers in characterizing AC Transit as a "fleet of buses that are dirty, poorly maintained and increasingly dangerous." In 1987, seventeen students were injured in a three-bus accident caused by faulty breaks. In 1989, AC Transit's reputation was severely damaged again when a bus full of children caught on fire and burned to the ground.

While firms like AC Transit have been quick to claim that issues like high rates of absenteeism are symptoms of worker behavior and individual characteristics, transit operators generally attributed their absences to work/life conflicts, stress, and pain. AC Transit, nevertheless, has been convinced that, despite problems with equipment and concerns with stressful working conditions, absentee rates and other issues were ultimately the result of worker misconduct. In its politics, this transit firm chose to overlook known workplace hazards and constraints that undermined the productivity of workers who have dependent relatives. AC Transit's management began to focus on the "the other side" through the implementation of workplace rules and practices that forced workers to show up to work, despite the personal and familial challenges they faced.

Management's Focus on "the Other Side": The Rise of Worker-Centered Bureaucratic Reforms

> When we took over, bus drivers and people in the trenches were way underpaid. They were below scale. But now they're up there. . . . It's a stressful job, but it doesn't require a lot of education and everything. . . . The emphasis is on the other side [more] now than before, especially the work rules . . . [that involve] absenteeism and the ability to not even show up . . . [or] call in.
>
> —Robert Nisbet, Former AC Transit Council and General Manager

After being forced to change the demographic makeup of its workplace, AC Transit began taking steps to improve perceived character flaws within the workplace through bureaucratic interventions designed to curtail concerns ranging from preventable accidents to customer complaints and high rates of absenteeism. As Nisbet recalls,[10] management no longer had to contend with complaints about poor job quality because AC Transit operators were among the highest paid operators in the nation.[11] AC Transit also received national recognition for its equipment maintenance as the recipient of the Fleet Owner Maintenance Efficiency Award from 1961 to 1979.[12] While setting national standards in mass transit operations and contending with racial and gender-specific disparities in their hiring and promotion norms, AC Transit created worker-centered rules that put the attention on "the other side." Frank Johnson, a Bus Maintenance Manager who had been with Key System since 1947 and retired from AC Transit in 1999, contended that when AC Transit was forced to hire African American women workers as transit operators and more racial minorities throughout the firm, the company did not view them as desirable workers.[13] As he put it,

> AC Transit continued to expand, and it continued to work very efficiently, but as we went along, as we lost people, the people that we were receiving to replace them were, I think, hired from the unemployable lines. We were not allowed—[to reject workers] . . . , it was an act of Congress. You were taken down to the personnel department, and they wanted to find out why this person was not acceptable. Here again, they were pushing, I know, to put minorities in. . . . But we were not allowed to screen out the minorities that didn't want to work, didn't care to come to work, or just plain didn't know anything, and to get the minorities that were really capable of doing this . . . they did have their quota, and they came in and they would announce to us that "thou shalt hire, train, and retain these people." All of a sudden, as the employment evolved, we were being hurt quite badly.

AC Transit managers were not alone in thinking the worst of the incoming transit operators. Various transit districts actively recruited from welfare-to-work programs and stated that their problem was selecting the best candidates among available workers, who had the right attitude, and the right skill level for the job. Transit operating proved to be difficult for workers transitioning from welfare to work to split shifts, fluctuating schedules, and a challenging work environment. This type of work presents a challenge because many transit operators, themselves, often rely on public transit to get to work, and frequently have difficulties balancing the responsibilities between work and family.[14]

No Time to Lean: Removing Breaks from the Workday

In order to contend with perceived shifts in the quality of workers hired throughout the company, AC Transit made various efforts to create rules and practices designed to ensure worker productivity that began in 1975 and intensified in the early 1980s. One of the first efforts made by AC

Transit to improve the productivity of its workforce came from its attempts to restructure break norms throughout the workday for operators assigned to the Dial-a-Ride program. Once Dial-a-Ride services began in Richmond, California, in 1975, AC Transit issued a policy bulletin to the Transportation Department stating that spot time (10-07), as presently practiced, negatively affected "efficiency and productivity." Previously, employees had been free to take a twenty-minute break every three hours by calling to the control room and stating "10-07." However, since the contract was silent on the matter of employee breaks, AC Transit attempted to discontinue this practice in order to improve quality of service available to Dial-a-Ride patrons. ATU 192 challenged this action because of an understanding between department supervisors and employees that 10-07 would be upheld, especially since AC Transit had previously recognized this practice. Due to AC Transit's refusal to rescind Bulletin 2-75, ATU 192 was compelled to appeal this decision through arbitration.[15]

Since the provisions for spot time (Code 10-07) in the collective bargaining agreement did not apply to the Dial-a-Ride operations, the union claimed that AC violated the agreement between division managers and employees that Dial-a-Ride operators would have access to spot time. ATU 192 admitted that the Dial-a-Ride operation differed from regular lines because it did not end at a specific location that would afford operators the breaks typical on a regular line. However, ATU 192 maintained that since the collective bargaining agreement was silent on this issue, previous practices should prevail.

After hearing both sides of the debate, Arbitrator William Eaton argued that Dial-A-Ride operators should have access to break time during the workday. Therefore, according to the arbitration ruling, both parties agreed that Dial-a-Ride drivers would be scheduled one thirty-minute break during a shift, and that operators on a split shift would receive this break as near as possible to the midpoint of their 3.5 or 4 hour shift.[16]

The Hits Keep Coming: AC Transit Introduces Pay Progression Scales

In the 1970s, ATU 192 members had become accustomed to winning rich contracts and generous fringe benefits. However, in the negotiation of their new labor contract in 1978, union leaders, including President John

Wesley Jr. met with strong resistance from AC Transit in the face of union wage improvement demands. In the face of the company's hard line, ATU 192 began a sixty-nine-day bus strike.

At a union meeting on January 15, 1978, ATU 192 members gathered to vote on their new contract proposal. Members claimed that the summary of the proposed contract was "vague" and did not provide the details necessary for progress in contract negotiations. Concerned Members 192, charged ATU 192 officials with discouraging discussion prior to the vote. Concerned Members 192, emerged within Local 192 as a group of workers disappointed by the "lack of democracy" within the union as demonstrated by the union officials' refusal to allow anyone to have "the right to voice their opinions and/or ask questions before a vote is taken."[17]

To remedy these problems, the Concerned Members called for ATU 192 leadership, now primarily consisting of African American men, to schedule an open dialogue at which union officials would present a plan detailing how the union intended to include the full membership in the quest to win the strike. Workers were against the proposed contract because, in their view, union officials were cooperating with management's attempts to scale back previous gains. For instance, the Concerned Members argued that they had "fought for and won [their] sick leave." However, AC Transit was currently in the practice of limiting this benefit by refusing to pay workers for their first day of sick leave. Under the proposed contract, workers would not be guaranteed sick leave pay until their third day on the sick book. Considering these developments, the Concerned Members contended that "it seems like we are going in the wrong direction." They went on to argue that "if things are really so tough that we can't get any improvement in our former contract, then let's at least keep what we had before. In any event, we should never give up any gains we have struggled for in the past, whether they be economic or improvements in working conditions. . . . We are not "hungry" and we are not "tired." Our spirits are high and we are madder than hell."

Concerned Members 192 were especially opposed to the new-hire progression schedule that would deflate the average compensation for ATU 192 members, once the top paid operators in the country. The 1975 contract had opened the door to the pay progression by allowing new hires to receive 12 percent less than the base rate for the first six months and 6 percent less for the next six months. Under the January 15 proposal, new hires would receive 30 percent less than the base pay for a year and would not gain access to the base pay until the third year. Put another way, under the old contract new hires stood to make $17,480 a year, but they would only make $13,455 if the January 15 version of the contract was ratified.

The Concerned Members 192 warned that this pay progression would not only hurt new hires but also current workers, noting that "AC can simply hire large numbers of new employees at the reduced rate of pay and use them instead of allowing us overtime. Less overtime in the last five years of work means less pay. Less pay for that period means a lower pension. . . . It is then true [that] present employees will be affected by the new progression. In fact, we will pay heavily for it!!"

After much debate within the union and convincing on the part of union officials, the strike ended late in January after members ratified a contract proposal on January 27, which gave bus drivers $.32 more than they were earning prior to the work stoppage. The ratified contract also required future AC Transit employees to wait much longer than previous AC employees before receiving top pay. The former contract stipulated a twelve-month progression; the January 1978 contract required a thirty-month pay progression to top pay.[18]

Curbing Attendance Trends through Bureaucratic Measures

In addition to reducing wages of newly hired workers, based on the company's perceptions of African American women and its concern with the rise of absenteeism within the workplace, many of the bureaucratic interventions created to manage worker's cultural capital revolved around improving attendance trends. Beginning in 1975, AC Transit began a new attendance program that cited operators for not reporting to work. The union and AC Transit agreed that the employer would cite the operators for "failure to report" as opposed to "refusal to report" as a way to avoid an insubordination charge; however, AC Transit did not implement this policy uniformly. Some operators were cited for failure to report and received a light penalty, while others, who were thought to be guilty of "refusing" to report received heavy penalties and were terminated. To make matters worse, AC Transit also acknowledged that it failed to inform employees of this policy when it chose to implement it.

After reviewing AC Transit's implementation of its attendance policy, Labor Arbitrator William Eaton found that AC's unilateral adoption of the new policy did not violate the union contract because it is the employer's "right to adopt reasonable rules, unless there are specific provisions in the agreement which preclude him from so doing, or which would require negotiation of such rules." At the same time, since AC Transit conceded that it failed to provide notice to employees, Eaton supported the firm's offer to publish a bulletin that outlined the system of discipline that related to miss-outs.[19] While the arbitrator considered the district's attendance policy to be "justifiable and reasonable," he wrote that "to be effective, the schedule of penalties to be assessed must be known beforehand." He ordered that AC Transit modify its attendance policy by giving workers "effective notice" and issuing two warning letters prior to suspension. Moreover, since he thought that "suspensions of three, four, and five days, coming to a total of twelve days, and to lost wages in excess of $600, amount to a rather extreme penalty,"[20] AC Transit was ordered to pay all operators who were suspended over seven days two days' back pay.[21]

Union archives reveal that ATU 192 and AC Transit went to arbitration again in 1988 to resolve a disagreement regarding AC Transit's continued practice of unfairly disciplining workers for unproductive work habits, in particular absenteeism.[22] Arbitrator Cohn in 1988 ruled AC Transit's absence control policy unreasonable because it considered total days of absence while ignoring mitigating circumstances. Although workers supplied managers with medical verification, forms were not kept with attendance records, nor were workers told they needed medical verification.[23] AC Transit was ordered to discontinue this policy and remove all discipline based solely on its attendance-control policies.[24]

Although AC Transit's Absence Control Program was struck down in May 1988 by Arbitrator Cohn, by December 16, 1988, AC Transit still had not reviewed the employee files to determine who had been unfairly impacted by the Absence Control Program.[25] This continued even after an October 28 meeting between the two organizations wherein AC Transit promised to review cases. AC Transit did not rescind the discipline and pay back wages of most workers affected by the Absence Control Program until March 1989.[26] The district proposed to rescind discipline and issue back pay to twelve workers, 60 percent of whom were African American and whose discipline was "primarily based on the ACP and therefore will not likely clear the hurdle Arbitrator Cohn's decision requires."[27] Meanwhile, workers like Judith Castellanos, a White female operator, did not get their jobs back without a fight. Operator Castellanos was dismissed for seven weeks for excessive absences during her pregnancy. She was reinstated without back pay because her absences were due to medical problems, but she had to go through arbitration to have her job reinstated.[28]

Factors Shaping Attendance Trends

The Issue of Occupational Stress

When faced with criticism from the public regarding declines in service, AC Transit's management and public relations consultants tended to attribute AC's service disruptions and rampant absenteeism to lack of employee commitment.[29] At the same time, most transit operator interviewees attributed these to industrial injuries and a more stressful, less rewarding job experience. Ruth, who handles scheduling and has thirty years of experience with AC Transit, claims this occurred over the last twenty years. In fact, as a transit operator she would say, "I can't wait until I get my time in so that I can work 3 or 4 hours and then get paid for 10 or 12." "But," she goes on, "that doesn't exist [anymore]. These Black men and women driving these buses right now are earning their money. They are earning every dime."

Not only do transit operators report being paid less for more work, they also face a time crunch. According to Shirley, a transit operator with AC for eighteen years, "it's not enough time, and the drivers are not able to do some of the things you need to do. Before you didn't have to be in such a rush. Now, you have to get from point A to B in X amount of minutes." Many also noted stressful encounters with patrons and traffic.

According to Georgia,

> People have problems with outside stuff and bring it on the bus; they may snap at you; they may mess with somebody else on the bus. Another stress is the traffic out there. People are not driving like they are supposed to. You know, everybody thinks that they have the right a way. They want to jump in front of you, get out on the side, bank on your bus; they want to turn across 2, 3, or 4 lanes to make a turn right in front of you . . . it's just a whole lot of stuff that you've got to trip on when you are out here. You've got to drive the bus, watch the traffic, and answer questions when people get on the bus. They want to know where this is at, and where that is at. They also start breaking down some of their personal problems, and you know, you don't want to hear all of that, but they do. And that's just some of the shit we go through.

Due to these pressures, researchers have reported high rates of absenteeism within the urban transit industry in addition to high turnover rates and high rates of early disability retirement that are caused by physical and environmental hazards in the work environment.[30] Researchers have also correlated the duration of bus driving with bad health, gastrointestinal disorders, and sleeping problems.[31]

Despite the increasing prevalence of workplace hazards throughout the 1970s and 1980s, ATU 192 spent a great deal of its time advocating for seniority rights rather than addressing the quality of work itself. However, by the late 1980s, seniority no longer carried the same weight, especially with regard to shift preference because the prime runs had been significantly modified or eliminated. Among the prime runs that were available in the past, split shifts would be one run (shift) assigned to a twenty- to twenty-five-year employee. In the end, both full-time and part-time workers are disadvantaged by this change in scheduling employees. Workers currently working eight-hour runs, could no longer look forward to the prime runs because they have been converted to part-time shifts. Meanwhile, the part-time worker's earning capacity was undermined by the short block of time they are not on the clock because this time off did not enable them to work another job.[32]

Although the use of part-time workers changed the nature of the job, transit employers were motivated by declining state and federal funds to cut costs that went beyond laying off workers. As an alternative to increasing fares, reducing bus maintenance costs, and eliminating service, many transit companies turned to part-time labor as an attempt to reduce operating costs during the lean years. Despite the fact that using part-time labor was controversial, this method of improving operating costs became a widely used employment practice by the early 1980s. Many transit companies at this time found that part-time labor helped reduce operating costs by requiring lower wages and fringe benefits and also helped to improve schedule efficiency, which is defined by the ratio of hours paid to hours worked.

The first large transit district to win the right to utilize part-time operators was the Seattle Metro in 1971. By 1981, the number of transit companies using part-time labor increased to more than half of the American Public Transit Association's membership, and by 1985, almost all of the American Public Transit Association member transit companies had obtained the right to use part-time operators. Having part-time labor at their disposal, management had the ability to assign short segments of a shift during a peak period to workers that cost less than their full-time counterparts. Management's adoption of this change in the labor process, however, was confronted with intense opposition from labor unions who believed that part-time operators were threats to victories secured on behalf of full-time workers. By introducing part-time labor, transit companies cut into a long-standing advantage in this profession, which involves the guarantee of a full day's pay, despite the midday lull of service.[33] For instance, an operator with two three-hour peak assignments would also be paid during the two hours that service is slow. During this time, research indicates that transit operators were not the only workers to see their workdays change to resemble "shift work," which is a job schedule that is different from the standard 8 A.M. to 5 P.M. workday.[34] In 1986, only 22 percent of workers engaged in shift work.[35] By 1991, the percentage of employees working this type of schedule increased to 45 percent.[36]

Unions fought management regarding its use of part-time workers by seeking limits on the amount and type of work part-time operators would be permitted to perform. For instance, they sought to make sure that the wage difference between part-time and full-time operators remained intact by stipulating that part-time workers would not be allowed to work more than an average of twenty-eight hours. Unions also fought to restrict transit companies' access to short shifts that were available on charter routes, holidays, and weekends.[37]

A transit manager in Chomitz et al.'s study noted the benefit of using part-time operators was that it gave management more time to screen workers and in a sense, extend the probation period. But, it turns out that turning to part-time labor did not achieve cost savings for transit firms because part-time workers had higher rates of absenteeism than full-time workers, mainly because the work hours were too hectic for those with young children and those who depended on other jobs to make ends meet. Although a supervisor in Chomitz et al.'s study noted that "once they have the uniform on, there's no way to distinguish a PTO from a full-time operator," there were workers who could not survive the work schedules.[38]

Nonetheless, transit districts like AC Transit gave this strategy of employing more women into part-time jobs another fighting chance. Although the number of African American men hired to work as a transit operator declined from forty-seven in 1981 to twenty-nine in 1985, the number of African American women hired on a part-time basis more than doubled from fourteen in 1981 to thirty-five in 1985. These part-time jobs were not a basis of mobility for the newly hired women. The only full-time transit operators hired between 1981 and 1985 entered the job primarily by transfer. This is especially the case among African American men in 1981 and African American women by 1985.

African Americans were not the only part-time workers whose mobility was blocked. White workers employed as full-time transit operators also gained these positions primarily via transfers from another department. White women transit operators working full-time experienced the least decline in the number of full-time positions throughout this time. While White women transit operators in 1981 only lost one full-time position and only six full-time positions by 1985, Black women transit operators lost three full-time slots in 1981 and by 1985 twenty-seven full-time positions.[39]

By the late 1980s, the run structure, especially from the union's and the worker's perspective changed for the worse. Despite the union's effort to minimize the effect of part-time labor on full-time employees, the use of part-time operators still affected full-time workers by limiting the type of shifts available to full-time workers because there were fewer runs with premium pay and overtime.[40] Prior to this time, the run would be a straight seven hours with an opportunity to work a "frag run" which guaranteed workers an additional three hours.[41] Frag runs, by the late 1980s, were starting to become attached to seven-hour runs. Instead of paying workers for 10 hours for work behind the wheel, due to the new run structure, AC Transit was paying workers for 8.5 hours for doing the same amount of work (i.e., working 10-hour shifts) they did under the previous run structure. Meanwhile, as pressures mount for drivers, especially those who are aware that they are being paid less to work more than previous generations of AC Transit operators, for many, the non-existent recovery time is a big problem. Although recovery time is included in a schedule, transit operators rarely have time to use it because their days often are unpredictable.

AC Transit continued to pursue bureaucratic interventions designed to curb absenteeism since AC Transit's absenteeism rate was "four times worse than its best peer and twice as bad as the average."[42] AC Transit continued to publicize its efforts to boost "driver morale," including slight adjustments to bus schedules. These proposals, however, did not entertain ways to improve work and family conflicts or address factors that negatively impacted workers' health both on and off the job.

Just as AC Transit began to proclaim that the lack of adequately motivated workers was preventing it from being a model mass carrier, AC Transit was forced to address occupational injury and its effect on absentee rates. In 1983, five AC Transit bus drivers filed a lawsuit against the mass transportation carrier for back problems caused by Anchorlok seats in the district's new coaches assembled by Gillig Corporation in Hayward, California. In November 1981, AC Transit purchased 131 "New Look" coaches from Gillig Corporation.[43] In 1983, AC Transit ordered another 134 coaches. According to the 1984 annual report, "the close proximity of the manufacturer had proved a boon in an earlier contract through reduction of delivery charges and improved response time in case of modifications and improvements requested by the District."[44]

The Gillig and Neoplan buses came equipped with the Anchorlok seat.[45] From the start, transit operators complained that the seats caused back, hip, and leg problems. As a result, numerous industrial injury claims were filed. These claims and concerns regarding the design, materials, and workmanship of Anchorlok seats, however, did not prompt AC Transit to remove the buses from service.

Lucille Jackson is one of the operators whose experience with the seats did not improve with modest adjustments. When Jackson first drove a bus with an Anchorlok seat in 1983, she missed work for two weeks due to seat-related injuries. The second time she drove a bus with an Anchorlok seat in 1986, she was in such pain she had to be carried off the bus and was unable to return to work the next day. Her last encounter with this seat contributed to lower back and right leg pain that made exiting the coach difficult at the end of her run.[46]

Doubt in AC Transit's desire to remedy this problem emerged among workers and the union just after the problems with the seats began. In a June 15, 1983, letter addressed to AC Transit Board Director Michael J. Fajans regarding the occupational health and safety problems caused by the inferior structural design of the Anchorlok seats, ATU 192 Union President Albert C. Johnson contended that "the attitude of management has been one of very little concern about the problem." Workers and the union continued to doubt AC Transit's commitment to fixing this problem because the district persisted in delaying the replacement of the Anchorlok seats, even after receiving approval by the AC Transit board of directors to move along with the process of purchasing the replacement seats in 1987.[47]

The continued use of these seats inevitably led to differences in sick leave and industrial injury trends within AC Transit. Driver absentee records by division point to large disparities in the number of workers absent due to sick leave and industrial injury. Table 4.1, which shows absentee trends by division and year between 1983 and 1986, illustrates that workers in East Oakland's Division 4, which is known as the "Black District," consistently called out more than other divisions due to a physical ailment or industrial injury. While nineteen employees in Division 4 were not working because of industrial injury, only two drivers in Division 6 (Newark/Hayward), which primarily housed high-seniority White male workers, could not work due to industrial injury. Although the number of workers out due to industrial injury declined in 1986, large disparities among the divisions remained.

The seat issue was not corrected until ATU 192 filed a grievance in 1987 claiming that AC Transit violated the collective bargaining agreement by requiring bus drivers to operate buses with Anchorlok seats. The labor union argued that the district's use of Anchorlok seats did not comply with applicable state statutes and regulations. Despite persistent complaints about the seats, AC Transit still used 194 buses with Anchorlok seats in 1987.[48]

Notwithstanding their continuous use of these buses, AC Transit did concede at the arbitration hearing in 1987 that the "Anchorlok seats caused injury to some drivers."[49] The district admitted that as the result of the seat's inadequate height adjustment, the seat did not provide adequate back support, especially for short drivers. AC Transit initially attempted to argue that many of the injured transit operators did not have a history of previous back pain, including workers considered "short." The problem with AC Transit's take was that it was inconsistent with the concerns brought by injured workers. For instance, the primary grievant, Operator Lucille Jackson, did not have a previous history of back pain and did not have an automobile accident prior to reporting her injuries. She recalled having to sit on the front edge of the seat because she was 5'3" tall and could not reach the brake and accelerator. Although she reported to her supervisor that she did not believe that she could drive the bus safely, she was instructed to continue her run. At the end of her shift, her back was aching and her right leg had become numb.[50]

Table 4.1 Number of workers absent by type, division, and year, 1983 and 1986

| | Year and Type of Absence | | | | | |
| | 1983 | | | 1986 | | |
Divisions	Sick Leave	Industrial Injury	No Call/ Show	Sick Leave	Industrial Injury	No Call/ Show
Emeryville-Div 2	32.5	6	3.9	24.4	4.3	2.4
Richmond-Div 3	16.1	8.2	1.7	18.5	9.7	1.8
E. Oakland-Div 4	41.3	19.3	5.8	40.1	12.9	6.2
Newark-Div 6	7	2.4	0.7	13.5	1.6	0.9

Source: Amalgamated Transit Union, Local 192 Records: 1983—"Drivers Weekdays Absenteeism Statistics, Reporting Period March 27, 1983–April 23, 1983," and 1986—"Drivers Weekdays Absenteeism Statistics, Reporting Period March 23, 1986–April 19, 1986."

While the seat had an immense impact on shorter drivers, tall transit operators assigned to drive Gillig buses with Anchorlok seats also experienced physical problems. Operator Vickers, a 6′2″ tall male transit operator reported that the seats caused lower back problems as well as pain in both legs. When he sought treatment for this pain at Kaiser, he received time off from work and appropriately eight months of medication with rest. Operator Kolar was 5′11″ and testified at the Jackson arbitration hearing that she also had to contend with problems caused by the Anchorlok seat. Operator Kolar reported that she began to develop pain inside her right shoulder blade because she had to "brace her left knee on the steering wheel column to hold herself in the seat."[51]

The district did eventually admit that inadequate lumbar support created a pressure behind drivers' knees. Seats also stressed the back due to intense vibration that sent shocks to the driver's spine. Due to these defects in seat design, AC Transit paid industrial injury claims of almost $220,000 for approximately fifty to sixty drivers and expected to pay an additional $88,600 due to injury claims attributed to the Anchorlok seats. Accordingly, the district filed a lawsuit against Lear Siegler, Inc., the manufacturer of the Anchorlok seats and Gillig Motor Coaches as well as the Neoplan Motor Coaches, the companies from which the district purchased the buses, due to AC Transit's evidence that the buses caused worker injury.[52]

AC Transit lost the arbitration and was required to replace all the Anchorlok seats and post notifications informing employees of their right to report pain or problems caused by seats while on duty. Furthermore, AC Transit was required to spread its buses with Anchorlok seats evenly across the district. AC Transit did not make the required adjustments and complete the retrofit of 212 coaches until over a year after losing the driver's seat arbitration.[53]

The Impact of Work/Life Conflicts within AC Transit

While most workers spoke candidly about their stressful work conditions and the reality of contending with AC Transit's new work rules, all mentioned that their struggle to keep the job has been shaped by this firm's slow response to work/life conflicts that include everything from ill-fitting uniforms to child care issues and their lack of access to clean restrooms while working. The union's priorities as they relate to protecting high-seniority workers did not alter significantly after African American women transit operators and other previously excluded workers began working for AC Transit in large numbers. With the exception of attendance policy complaints and disputes concerning employees being forced to work out of their classification as well as the addition of contract clauses that acknowledged the workers' right to clean restrooms and adequate breaks, ATU 192 limited their advocacy and arbitration efforts in the workplace to issues that negatively impacted high-seniority workers. As a result, the union regularly engaged in labor management disputes regarding the seniority rights of workers attempting to secure overtime and better shifts, while overlooking issues that were of particular relevance to women workers, who seemed to be much less of a priority to the union and AC Transit.[54]

For instance, both AC Transit and ATU 192 were so far removed from making efforts to accommodate women's presence on the job that these organizations neglected to make sure that uniforms were altered to adjust for differences in men's and women's bodies. In response, many women made efforts to adjust their issued uniforms by replacing the ties with scarfs and purchasing fabric to create pants that fit them while they were busy at work. It was a significant gain for women when the union negotiated that women could wear culottes on the job. Before this right was won, women transit operators had to wear men's pants or risk being written up for not wearing the uniforms issued to them. This work rule was unfair to women transit workers because, as Christine Zook, former ATU 192 president–business agent recalls, uniforms designed for men "were straight up and down and just didn't work."[55]

Child Care Problems

In addition, until the late 1990s, minimal efforts were made to help workers with dependent relatives balance work and family responsibilities because the workers who previously held these positions were older men who did not have to balance dependent care responsibilities with work. Although ATU 192 has attempted to include child care provisions in the contract since 1983,[56] concerted efforts to provide necessities like child care did not emerge until women secured key leadership roles within AC Transit and ATU 192 and began to designate the work culture and the conflicts it presents as areas for reform. Since the new hires in the post–Affirmative Action era primarily worked split shifts, many did not have child care available in the morning and began addressing their work/life balance concerns by allowing their children to ride with them on the bus.[57] Others solved the problem by missing work.

A survey conducted in 1989 by Netsy Firestein, the executive director of the Labor Project for Working Families, indicated that many of their respondents, who were AC Transit and San Francisco Muni drivers, had a tough time juggling their work and family responsibilities. This survey was the first effort to highlight the extent to which child care issues among transit operators impacted their ability to work. Once more women gained access to positions of power within AC Transit and ATU 192, interest in child care responsibilities reemerged. One of the first actions by the Dependent Care Committee was to replicate the 1989 survey in 1996 in order to determine the extent to which child care issues still impacted AC Transit operators. In this survey, respondents reported that a great deal of their absences were caused by their inability to solve child care issues. For instance, during a two-month period, 21 percent of respondents did not go to work because their child's center or school closed, 23 percent of respondents missed work because their child care arrangements fell apart, and 43 percent of respondents missed work because of a sick child.[58]

These results motivated individuals within AC Transit that were interested in work/life balance including the new ATU President Christine Zook and the general manager at the time, Sharon Banks. Although the dependent care committee formed and met regularly to discuss these concerns, efforts were not made by AC Transit and ATU to address this matter until five years after the 1996 survey. Then, without much opposition from management, workers secured various benefits in their 2001 contract that were designed to address the child care issues including extended leave, allowing workers to take sick leave in hourly increments, and creating a dependent care trust fund to which AC Transit contributes $.03 for every hour worked by ATU members.[59]

Access to Clean Restrooms

Meanwhile, although women transit operators did eventually gain access to more suitable uniforms and access to family friendly provisions in their contract, they continue to have difficulty gaining access to clean restrooms while at work. Despite the fact that access to clean bathrooms and time to use them have been an important health and safety concern since African American women began working as operators in large numbers and the recent efforts of transit labor organizations successfully advocating for adequate rest periods for operators to be recognized by the State of California in 2001,[60] problems persist. Although many drivers, especially women, have brought up this issue, ATU 192 did not begin to push aggressively for clean rest rooms and time to use them until the late 1980s, years after the right to sanitary restrooms and adequate spot time was first acknowledged in the labor contract, effective July 1, 1974.[61] However, as a result of AC Transit's tight run schedules and rules that punished workers for disrupting service for a restroom break in addition to the union's lengthy silence on this issue,[62] transit operators, especially those who are women, have developed health problems. An AC transit operator survey in 2003 that identifies the need for adequate restroom breaks as a critical concern among these workers also indicates that women are more likely to contend with urinary tract infection than men due to the lack of access to adequate restroom breaks while at work.[63]

This matter involving the accessibility of sanitary restroom facilities did not begin to improve until women began to gain leadership positions within ATU 192 and within AC Transit. The union and AC Transit first recognized its joint obligation to ensure that workers are provided clean restroom breaks in the 1998 contract, while under the leadership of Christine A. Zook and Claudia Hudson, the president and vice president of ATU 192, due to the finding of a 1997 survey that demonstrated that operators' health and stress levels would be improved by providing adequate restroom facilities.[64] By 2008, while under the leadership of Yvonne Williams, president–business agent of ATU 192, transit operators were still attempting to secure the appropriate time allotted for meal and rest provisions and were forced to secure these rights through the arbitration process.[65] Although they eventually won access to adequate bathroom breaks, in 2010, ATU 192 members were involved in another dispute with AC Transit regarding restroom breaks with regard to its concerns about unsanitary conditions within the restrooms that AC Transit made available to workers. While an arbitrator in 2010 ruled that AC Transit provide its workers restrooms with sanitary conditions, concerns regarding the firm's compliance with this ruling exist because, as union members put it, "bosses often seem to have no concept of what is 'suitable' or 'sanitary.'"[66] As such, their fight to secure sanitary restroom conditions continues.

Impact of Strained Labor-Management Relations

As working conditions soured, AC Transit workers in various departments including transportation as well as clerical departments began to file grievances regarding workload and run structure disputes in the early 1980s. Throughout this period, the district made willful attempts to violate sections of the collective bargaining agreement. In some instances, it used gaps in the contract to justify unilateral actions. ATU 192 filed grievances that addressed these problematic shifts in the work process including excessive split shifts and the declining number of straight through runs with Saturdays and Sundays off in addition to the union's persistent claim of inadequate restroom facilities and the insufficient time to use those facilities.

Labor disputes continued to mount by 1985 and most of these grievances were penned by union attorney Alan Kopke. On behalf of ATU 192, Kopke filed various grievances that challenged unilateral shifts made by the district that affected the terms and conditions of employment. The specific violations included (1) the transfer of work from one division to another, (2) forcing workers to work beyond their classification, (3) failure to consult the union prior to transferring work from one division to another and assigning new work duties, (4) failure to provide adequate job descriptions for clerical and office positions, and (5) assigning work out of classification with disregard to proper pay and bid procedures.[67] Further grievances centered on pay, work assignments, seniority rights, and concerns regarding disability accommodations. In one case involving wrongful termination, an AC Transit operator Russell Stover was injured while on duty. Stover was then for a short time assigned to the Research and Planning Department due to his physical disability. Later AC Transit terminated Mr. Stover due to this disability. Labor Attorney Alan Kopke wrote to AC Transit Attorney Dan Ready that ATU 192 contested that AC Transit violated contract sections 85.08 and 90.03 by not paying Mr. Stover according to his seniority when he began his nondriving assignment and did not allow him to use his seniority to bid for positions in the Clerical Department that could accommodate his disability. ATU 192 called for Mr. Stover's reinstatement, full back pay, and that the district make reasonable efforts to accommodate his disability in addition to other similarly situated workers included in the grievance.

ATU 192 and AC Transit met on November 1, 1985, to discuss the twenty-eight terminations, including Mr. Stover's, due to medical problems. The union provided the district with a nine-page proposal that it believed constituted a basis for settlement. In response to this proposal, AC Transit's attorney Daniel Ready commented that the union's proposal had "one or more meritorious suggestions," but he vehemently argued against the assertion that it was required by contract to reasonably accommodate anyone who could not perform the work due to physical ailments. Ready further contended that while the district was open to arbitration on the matter, it was not open to reinstating medical coverage since the workers in question were terminated and did not possess the right to medical coverage that is protected by the labor contract. Finally, he reported that eighteen of the twenty-eight terminated workers accepted severance pay, while at least another four more applied for disability pensions.[68]

ATU 192 also filed a grievance on behalf of AC Transit worker Sharon Cunningham who was terminated while on pregnancy leave. Two weeks before her discharge, Ms. Cunningham submitted a note from her doctor indicating that she was disabled "with severe heart palpitation and pregnancy" since May 16, 1985. While on pregnancy leave, Ms. Cunningham was required by her AC Transit supervisor, R. L. Cota, to report to work on July 12, 1985, to bring information from her physician. Although she claimed that she did not receive the notice, on August 1, 1985, Mr. Cota informed the union that Ms. Cunningham did not report as requested and that disciplinary charges were pending. The union submitted a request for a hearing on the charges on August 15, 1985, but Mr. Cota, the Division 4 superintendent, refused to hold a first-level hearing on the matter. Instead, he issued a letter stating that the union's request for a first-level hearing did not reach him until August 22, 1985. Due to this, Cota claimed that the grievance was moot because it was not submitted in a timely fashion.[69]

On the contrary, ATU 192 maintained that Cota failed to hold a timely first-level hearing and as a result the district violated the time limits of section 3.03 of the contract and forfeited its case. Despite these developments, ATU 192 requested that AC Transit schedule an appeal hearing or hold a late first-level hearing regarding Ms. Cunningham's case. According to its labor attorney, ATU 192 was not sure what motivated Mr. Cota to fire Ms. Cunningham. Furthermore, Kopke wrote "we do not know why he was so eager to strip her and the Union of their rights to a hearing on the ridiculous 'charge' of not reporting to work while off on disability." At the end of this correspondence, Kopke wrote that "we therefore await your call, A/C Transit."[70]

ATU 192 soon found that AC Transit would in this matter as well as others use excuses similar to the one employed in Mrs Cunningham's case to avoid taking corrective actions to address labor contract violations. In the case of Ms. Cunningham in addition to cases involving other workers, AC Transit made efforts to circumvent the grievance and arbitration procedures by claiming that the union made untimely requests. In response to this claim, the district canceled hearings on the premise that time limit violations are indisputable and do not require a forum for review. Instead of making the grievance process work, AC Transit began attempting to avoid the grievance and arbitration decisions by allowing managers to make decisions in letters as opposed to having issues debated in hearings provided through the grievance procedure.

ATU 192 made attempts to address this situation by filing grievances regarding the district's practice of discharging employees with industrial injuries. During this time, AC Transit started blocking ATU 192's ability to represent the workers by restricting access to documents crucial to their defense. When ATU 192 pursued cases that required access to medical and workers' compensation files, AC Transit developed a pattern of refusing to make the documents available to ATU 192, even when the documents were subpoenaed by the arbitrator. Cases involving Joe

Estrada and Preston Johnson led to ATU 192's attempts between 1979 and 1980 to force AC Transit to provide access to documents needed to represent workers. In Johnson's case, ATU 192 needed to show that other workers had similar accident records and were allowed to maintain their employment.[71] However, the arbitrator's award in this case declared that the documents they requested to support their argument in the Johnson case should not be available to the union until the statute of limitations ran out on claims against AC Transit concerning the incident. According to the arbitration award in the Johnson case, the union would not have access to accident summaries of other drivers, supervisor reports, courtesy cards, and police records until well after these documents could be used to assist workers facing termination of stiff punishments for breaking work rules. Based on their experiences attempting to gain access to documents, the union decided to pursue this matter in court. They hoped to get a judgment that would either force AC Transit to grant the union access to all documentation needed in the future or use the judicial determination to persuade arbitrators in future cases that they should have access to documentation.

ATU 192 also pursued a Dishonesty Grievance in response to AC Transit's supervisors' tendency to assume that workers filled out forms incorrectly or left out information were guilty of dishonesty, conduct that would lead to discharge. In response to this grievance, AC Transit agreed to circulate a bulletin to supervisors that explains the definition of dishonesty and how best to address it. In addition, ATU 192 filed a grievance regarding AC Transit's use of criminal arrests to determine hiring or promotion decisions. Due to Labor Code section 432.7, which prohibited employers from using arrest records when there were no subsequent convictions, ATU 192 maintained that AC Transit was improperly obtaining these records. The grievance was dropped after the district issued a statement that expressed its policy when current workers are arrested for conduct that occurs off the job.[72]

Impact of Internal Power Struggles within the ATU 192

Despite its efforts to advocate for workers, it is important to note that the effectiveness of ATU 192 and the culture of opportunity within AC Transit were also undermined by persistent internal power struggles within the union. Conflicts among union leaders and members began to mount by the mid-1970s and began compromising the nature of solidarity among the rank and file employed by AC Transit. As a result, African American men began to challenge White union leaders to address discriminatory workplace practices in lieu on focusing on pension and seniority rights disputes. These ATU 192 members believed that the union was failing them because they felt deprived of a voice in shaping the goals of the union. ATU 192's delay in stressing safety measures protecting workers against problems ranging from violence on the bus to the lack of well-maintained equipment contributed to the increasingly precarious nature of the job as well as shifts in the culture of opportunity in this workplace.

ATU 192 union members were especially bothered by the fact that despite the racial/ethnic composition shifts within the AC Transit workforce, the demographic makeup of union leadership remained the same. Efforts by the group Progress in Action an organization of African American male employees of AC Transit was directly involved in encouraging a shift in the demographic makeup of union leadership during the mid-1970s. This group, which consisted of five Division 4 African American male transit operators came together on Seminary Street in Oakland and decided to do something about their working conditions as well as their exclusion from positions of power within the union.[73] They began connecting to concerns of the workers employed by the district and the union by circulating a newsletter called the *"00" Express*. Due to their belief that their exclusion from leadership positions in the union was based on the color of their skin and not their commitment to the job, they vigorously advocated for change both through community efforts as well as through confrontations with management regarding the need to expand their access to supervisor positions. They also worked to make the union more inclusive by educating their fellow African American rank and file about their right to take an active role in the union. As a result of their efforts, which involved educating themselves about the union rules and how to use those rules to improve their standing within the union, African American men in particular finally gained access to union officer positions by the late 1970s. This group was also successful in getting more African American workers involved in union affairs. Meanwhile, although men of color secured high-level union positions over twenty years after AC Transit starting hiring, it took another twenty years before women got a chance to hold high-level leadership positions within the union. ATU 192 was the first transit union in the country to negotiate equal pay for women transit operators; however, it was delayed in acknowledging women's needs and leadership ability within the union.

The legacy of excluding African American men and women workers from leadership roles within the union sheds light on the disconnect between union leaders and workers, particularly with regard to how demographic shifts within the AC Transit workforce promoted a crisis of authority within the union that led White male leaders to fiercely defend challenges to their authority and delay in responding to the needs of the changing workforce that was gradually shifting from predominantly White male to predominately Black male and women workers. Research detailing the power struggles between the established White male leadership and the increasingly Black and female AC Transit workforce also support the contention that this labor organization had a tough time understanding and advocating for the needs of these workers. If this union was interested in developing a democratic stance that valued each member, union rules like those regarding seniority rights that were originally implemented for the purposes of establishing a hierarchy among union members needed to be revisited because these rules eventually began to have racial implications.

Instead, ATU 192's established seniority system, which helps establish workers' access to certain benefits including order of layoff and priority in bidding for a job, perpetuated prior discriminatory hiring and promotion policies of AC Transit. When the antidiscrimination clause was first added ATU 192's contract in 1974, which also details the district's obligation to develop job descriptions and how workers will be promoted into lower level management positions, all job rewards from days off to filling vacancies such as an assistant dispatcher or dispatcher are connected to seniority.[74] Section 44's Seniority Clause noted that "seniority shall prevail in selections of shifts, runs, day off and vacations. Reduction of force shall be in accordance to inverse seniority."[75] The seniority system restricted workers with less time on the job, namely, African American male and female workers, to their positions of origin and limited their capacity to move up in the firm because their length of service was based on time within a particular department as opposed to total service in all company positions. In turn, the seniority system was instrumental in perpetuating the underutilization of Black and female labor within AC Transit by requiring workers transferring to a preferred position to forfeit his or her seniority status earned in a previous department as if she or he just began working for the district.

Finally, the solidarity among ATU 192 workers was also challenged by competing factions within the union. One of the battles took place during the 1981 elections, wherein union officers I. P. Cordeiro and then President–Business Agent Richard K. Windrich were attempting to control the election battle with none other than attendance policies. "Chili" Garcia, "Moody" M. McMillian, and Jerry Sullivan, who were ATU 192 members vying for leadership positions within the union vigorously opposed these rules. They hired Attorney Henry J. Rodriguez to request that ATU 192 postpone the December 1981 elections in order to ensure that "valid nominations" are made in a general membership meeting. Attorney Rodriguez argued that while the requirement that members attend the six regular meetings during the twelve months prior to being nominated as a union officer was reasonable, he contended that using the attendance books violated the rights of union members because the attendance books were "deficiently kept" and were not accurate. Oftentimes, he wrote, the attendance book would not be available at a meeting to account for the members present. In response to the Rodriguez's correspondence received on November 23, I. P. Cordeiro, then financial secretary–treasurer of ATU 192 wrote that the election would not be postponed because the three workers involved in this complaint were not nominated at a Nominations Meeting held on November 2, 1981, "regardless of whether the Eligibility Committee may later find them ineligible."[76] A similar concern was voiced by Gene Wright who filed a lawsuit against ATU 192 on November 20, 1984, because the labor union concluded that he was ineligible to be elected as business agent. Mr. Wright requested to be reimbursed for election expenses and that the court restrained ATU 192 from excluding him from the election. Mr. Wright did not benefit from challenging the union. His request was also denied.[77]

Summary

While AC Transit eventually amended its hiring procedures in ways that diversified the workplace, evidence in this chapter demonstrate that AC Transit also responded to the new hiring demands by restructuring the labor process and creating worker-centered policies that profoundly altered the structure of opportunity available to transit operators. Evidence from interviews with transit operators as well as the archival data suggests that while African American women certainly made progress with AC

Transit, by the time they entered the field, the transit operating position had become less attractive to men and women, due to increasingly stressful work pressures. Evidence in this chapter also illustrates that instead of expanding opportunity, AC Transit developed a system of management that delegitimized the collective bargaining process and forced workers to increasingly engage in human resource policies designed to protect the firm from workers it perceives to be "inept" and "from the unemployable lines" who lack moral character and labor market commitment.

Instead of creating redistributive policies and norms within the workplace, AC Transit's symbolic compliance with antidiscrimination policies culminated into a series of policies that can be characterized as instances of covert discrimination, due to the disproportionate implementation of absence control rules as well as the unequal patterns of discipline and punishment. For various years, AC Transit publicly blamed service disruptions and faulty bus maintenance to Affirmative Action policies that forced them to hire "inept" or "unqualified" workers. To the contrary, evidence may be interpreted to suggest that service declines and high absentee rates were more likely caused by faulty equipment that increased the risk of occupational injury, work/life conflicts that the job process created, as well as the district's failure to uphold its high standard of servicing its vehicles.[78]

Evidence also suggests that the nature of labor relations between the firm and the labor union played a significant role in addressing social inequality within AC Transit throughout the period of study. During this time, management and labor relations became increasingly strained as management began to ignore workplace precedents and refuse to arbitrate and in some cases review worker concerns presented by labor union leaders. Evidence demonstrates that AC Transit developed a pattern of losing union grievances, eliminating the appeals process, and undermining the arbitration hearing procedures by refusing to comply with the arbitrator's binding ruling. Since their concerns on behalf of workers were being overlooked, labor unionists with ATU 192 began to enlist labor attorneys to write out grievances by the mid-1980s.

Lastly, this era in urban transit union history was one of retrogression, as characterized by an extended period of ineffective bargaining and the weakening of the democratic processes within the union as well as the workplace. Transit operators hired in the post–Affirmative Action era encountered a new era of unionism in the transit industry wherein mounting financial pressures on transit districts and continuing schisms within the union and membership resulted in shifts in the culture of opportunity within transit workplaces as well as changes in the nature of worker solidarity and bargaining priorities. This chapter illustrates how ATU 192's actions played a significant role in perpetuating social inequality due to the nature of their advocacy for African American women transit operators. ATU 192 did make efforts to mitigate disparities caused by deviations in workplace practices (Memorandum of Understanding 1975); however, this labor organization devoted much less effort to improving the status of these workers and opposing shifts in working conditions that undermined their ability to maintain their employment with AC Transit. While management and labor relations became increasingly strained, schisms within the union simultaneously undermined workers' confidence in the union's capacity to represent their concerns.

Since a dual unionism developed within AC Transit's post–Affirmative Action era workplace, wherein the issues nagging long-time members were addressed while the concerns of newly hired women union members were overlooked until concerted advocacy emerged, this chapter takes a closer look at the consequences of worker-centered reforms within AC Transit. The women transit operators employed by AC Transit are union members; however, the impact of their union membership pales in comparison to the time when the transit operator position was exclusive to White men. Chapter 5 captures what happens when dues-paying African American men and women transit operators are singled out by worker-centered as well as safety-specific reforms. In this chapter, I document how workers lost jobs, chronicle their attempts to win back their jobs, and present the sobering reality of gridlock, wherein workers are afforded an opportunity to confront their workplace hardships and struggles but nothing comes from their efforts due to the boost in employer autonomy and the decline in the union's capacity to protect its members from unfair and arbitrary workplace conditions. Monica, an AC Transit operator for eighteen years, contends that despite the union's efforts to advocate for workers, the structure of opportunity had been undermined primarily by the institutional assumptions and practices of AC Transit. As she put it,

> management to a certain extent is at a loss as to how to encourage or motivate employees to do the work . . . basically, there is a presumption by management that we are unskilled labor. They feel that most

of us that hold these jobs don't deserve to have it and couldn't go anywhere else . . . So the politics of it goes back to the impression of management as to the qualifications and abilities of most of the employees that are African American or minorities at this present time who have something in place called a collective bargaining agreement that really wasn't designed for them. It was designed for the good ole boys, who have retired. They deserved it, and we don't.

5

Drug Tests and Pencil Whippings

The Consequences of Workplace Discipline within AC Transit

In 2014, a television news report from Oakland's *WBRZ 2 Investigates*, revealed more trouble brewing between AC Transit and the transit operators who work for them. Transit operators had been receiving tickets for traffic violations, which were arriving by mail. Police had been issuing these $260 tickets to transit operators for stopping, even momentarily, to drop off or pick up passengers at a few of the BART stations in Oakland. Transit operators primarily affected by this were those whose runs required them to stop at the Lake Merritt BART station and the MacArthur BART station, as well as the West Oakland, Coliseum, and Rockridge BART stations. Most of the traffic citations occurred during busy commute times when transit operators found themselves needing to pause the vehicle briefly within restricted areas.

Frustrated transit operators in this news story complained about limited legal places to pick up and drop off patrons and contended that the Alameda County sheriff's deputies were being overly strict in their enforcement of parking restrictions. However, J. D. Nelson, spokesperson for the Alameda County Sheriff's Office maintained that the deputies were citing workers for good reason. As he put it, "if the issue is 'I was only there for five seconds and five seconds is okay,' then is ten seconds okay? Is fifteen seconds okay? Is thirty seconds okay? Is a minute okay? It doesn't say no parking for longer than five seconds, it says no parking." In the report, AC Transit's spokesperson Clarence Johnson explained that, to avoid tickets, transit operators simply needed to cease parking in any red zone, upholding the company's interest in protecting the public's safety. Parking in blocked zones, according to Johnson, is a safety hazard that may cause delays in service.

Nicole Huey, one of the transit operators who spoke with *2 Investigates*, complained that the rules had not been clear, especially in light of construction projects in the area, which necessarily affected parking and traffic options. According to Operator Huey, "the actual drop off station is way on the other side of all the construction that's taking place." 2 *Investigates* visited the other highly ticketed BART stations and found the same confusion. Many drivers who had been cited for illegally stopping in the red zone explained that the 8th Street traffic pattern lacked a clearly delineated white zone for dropping off and picking up patrons. Johnson suggested that transit operators drop patrons "many feet away from that [white] zone" to avoid the tickets. The Alameda County Sheriff's Office spokesperson addressed the transit operators, saying "you may have to circle around once or twice, but eventually you're going to have a spot that opens up. Sometimes people are in a hurry or they get lazy."

Because fines represented profit for AC Transit, it is hardly surprising that the sheriff's office and the transit company did not address the transit operators' concerns but instead defended the issuing of fines. AC Transit reported that it had taken in a few million dollars in revenue from parking citations. Receiving over one million dollars by the middle of fiscal year 2013–2014, AC Transit's total revenue from parking enforcement citations added up to almost $1.2 million. 2 *Investigates* reported that "officials say the county does not keep any of the money. Instead, it goes back to AC Transit." When transit operators receive a citation, the company refers them to the AC Transit website, which instructs them on how to contest a citation. If they are unsuccessful in contesting a citation, the fine goes into the coffers of the company.[1]

This 2 *Investigates* story may seem bizarre. But, this strict and punitive policy is consistent with broader patterns of social control within AC Transit as well as other transit districts across the United States. Transit workers in cities such as Chicago; Kenosha, Wisconsin; New York; and Baton Rouge, Louisiana, have been complaining about the many rules designed to control how workers perform and present themselves as mass transit operators. Among these rules are strict punishments, including discharge for a range of issues including cell phone use while on duty, excessive absences, and substance abuse. While workers have been terminated for skipping bus stops and not showing up to work due to personal emergencies in Baton Rouge, in New York City, workers represented by TWU 100 have been complaining about low wages and overly strict discipline. TWU 100 leaders contend that New York City transit operators, often suspended without a hearing, are presumed guilty and expected to prove their innocence at disciplinary proceedings. TWU leaders also report that transit companies are heavily disciplining workers for minor infractions, including "having three buttons open on a uniform shirt during a scorching summer day or wearing prohibited clothing, such as hooded sweat shirts, during the winter."[2]

This chapter explores the consequences of worker-centered reforms within AC Transit and uncovers the peculiar patterns of punishment that peaked between the mid-1970s to 2009. I draw from interviews with respondents to illustrate the disproportionate nature of workplace punishment. I also draw heavily from union archives to investigate cases in which workers objected to transit company policies as well as the Federal Transit Administration's audits of AC Transit's drug-testing program.

Pencil Whippings within AC Transit

Similar to fellow transit workers throughout the country, African American women transit operators whom I interviewed expressed a great deal of concern with what one African American woman firefighter called "pencil whipping," wherein supervisors persistently write up damaging information on a worker, creating grounds to say, "We tried to train her, but she is unable to effectively do her job."[3] Reba Gauer, a White woman transit operator who worked for National City Lines and then AC Transit for over thirty-two years, claimed she did not have a problem with supervisors. As she recalled, "never had any problems with supervisors. Never had any problems with superintendents, even. I worked under every superintendent they had. Never had any problems."[4]

In contrast, many African American women transit operators report that relations between drivers and supervisors have soured over time. As Barbara, an African American woman transit operator with ten years at AC Transit put it, "They are very nit-picky about different things. If you have on the wrong hat, you will get wrote up. If your shirt is out, you will get wrote up. All kinds of little different things can lead to being dismissed." Shirley lends evidence for this pattern, noting that she has been written up for wearing the wrong kind of shoes when the company did not furnish shoes. She also mentioned being written up for waving at a supervisor: for a brief moment, she had released both hands from the steering wheel, and for this she was being punished.

Many African American workers also formally complained about harassment and harsh, arbitrary punishment by AC Transit supervisors who seemed motivated by personal conflicts unrelated to work. For example, when facing discharge for insubordination, Operator Johnny Jackson attempted to defend himself and keep his job by claiming that

Supervisor Wardell Miles had been harassing him and would not leave him alone.[5] Jackson was written up for threatening Miles around 6 P.M. at the intersection of West and 40th Streets in Oakland, while Jackson was traveling eastbound on 40th Street and Miles was heading westbound on the same street. Miles reported that as they passed each other, Jackson stuck his head out of his bus window and stated that he was "going to get [his] ass." At his hearing, Jackson stated that Miles stood in front of the coach for several minutes before stating his reasons for confronting the transit operator. Then, when Miles stepped into the coach and said to Jackson, "I guess you know why I'm here," Jackson allegedly said, "No, I don't know and don't give a fuck." Jackson called the central dispatcher to report his discomfort with Miles's presence and asked to be relieved if the pressure from his supervisor did not end. Jackson was later relieved by Superintendent Jeffries because Miles told the superintendent that Jackson wanted relief.[6]

Throughout his hearing, Jackson maintained that he had not threatened Miles. Miles's accusation of a threat could only be referring to Jackson's comment that he [Jackson] would "make him [Miles] see the white man just like he [Miles] made me see the white man."[7] Jackson claimed that ultimately, Miles fabricated these threats and statements of insubordination. He clarified in his hearing, "I'm only trying to get you people to understand that Wardell Miles is out to have me fired because he has a little authority now and because he has a bad grudge against me."[8] Previously, the two men had pursued the same woman, and, according to Jackson, Miles was still upset about the outcome.

Jackson mentioned in the hearing that he just wished that this conflict did not play out at his job. As he put it, "I'd rather for him to just see me somewhere in the street and get it off, instead of coming on my job as far as having me suspended and losing time because I have a family just like [him]."[9] He went on to say, "the whole thing is [that] . . . I'm sorry to be in the office for something I haven't done, but yet and still I have got to clarify everything cause the way it is now, I'm the only one suffering. Wardell Miles is still working. . . . I don't like the fact that a supervisor comes out and harass[es] . . . the drivers catch all the hell out there anyway, not the supervisor, not the superintendent, not the general manager, but the driver. . . . They're the one[s] who catch the hell, and I don't think it's fair."[10]

In this case, AC Transit was unable to offer concrete evidence to prove that Jackson threatened Miles. Despite a total lack of proof of insubordination, however, the incident cost Jackson a twenty-eight-day suspension with no pay. For two years, Jackson attempted to get the punishment overturned through the grievance and appeal process, but his efforts were unsuccessful.[11]

In another case involving an insubordination charge, AC Transit discharged utility employee Gary Turner, who had worked for the company for just over two years. The discharge took place on February 14, 1983.[12] In the arbitration hearing, AC Transit claimed it discharged Turner because he refused to follow orders from his leadman and foreman to sweep a coach several weeks prior, on January 18.[13] Turner maintained that this duty had not been on his original task list and that when the leadman asked him to sweep the coach, he responded that he was unable to do so at that time because he was currently cleaning up a fuel spill. Since the district could not prove that Turner committed an act of "gross" insubordination, the arbitrator's award found the discipline imposed on Turner to be extreme. Turner was later reinstated with seniority and other company benefits but without back pay.[14]

Compared to the African American women transit operators I interviewed with less than three years on the job, those with more than three years of experience had a heightened awareness of discipline patterns and were more willing to discuss their impressions and concerns with me. Many of these women reported that the company's increased surveillance and punishment of African American employees for allegations of insubordination were not merely efforts to improve the quality of service or rid the mass carrier of disrespectful workers but were vehicles of discrimination. Georgia remarked, "You got supervisors out here trying to ride you for every little thing. Petty shit. But I think they do it because they are getting pressure from their boss. I believe that it is too many of us [African Americans] in here, and that they are trying to get rid of some of us." Monica, the union representative, had a different take on the reason for the shift back to what she calls a "plantation style of management." In her opinion, the scarcity of well-paying jobs available to all workers had a lot to do with this shift. According to Monica,

> The people that didn't want this job want it back. . . . [So] it's about the blue collar jobs leaving this country and even the White collar jobs in the high tech industry leaving this county. . . . What's left is a very slim picking that will afford you an annual salary where you can still realize your American dream, which is to buy a house, send

Table 5.1 Variations in discipline by division, 1984

Division	Average Discipline Score
Division 2-Emeryville	2.7 (1.66)
Division 3-Richmond	3.6 (1.34)
Division 4-East Oakland	3.3 (1.50)
Division 6-Hayward/Newark	1.5 (1.94)

$N=51$; standard deviation in parentheses.
Source: Amalgamated Transit Union Local 192, Records: "Discipline Pending at Division Six, July 31, 1984"; "Memo to Edgar Jackson, Appeal Hearings, Wednesday, May 2, 1984"; "Memo to Edgar Jackson, Appeal Hearings, Wednesday, May 9, 1984"; "Memo to Edgar Jackson, Appeal Hearings, Wednesday, April 25, 1984"; "Memo to Edgar Jackson, Appeal Hearings, Wednesday, April 12, 1984"; "Memo to Edgar Jackson, Appeal Hearings, Wednesday, April 17, 1984."

your kids to college, to have 1-point or 2-point whatever children [while] only work[ing] one job. We get antagonized a lot by certain communities, [and] Alameda is one of them, where people feel like you should be humbly grateful because they realize what your annual salary and hourly salary is, mostly because we talk too much, but other than that, the contracts are on the internet. They know that you have paid medical, that you have dental, that you have paid vacation, that you have a retirement plan here. These jobs, what we have here, they want them back.

Concerns regarding employment insecurities among the transit workers are not new. They began in 1975 with AC Transit's attendance control policy and the patterns of disparate punishment that emerged in the mid-1980s, as evidenced by Local 92 records. Table 5.1 reveals significant variation between divisions in terms of the average discipline of drivers. I derived these estimates from 1984 appeal hearing records, which I looked at by division and which record the names of workers written up, the nature of their infractions, and the proposed discipline. With estimates from the appeal hearing records, I coded discipline by type, using an ordinal variable ranging from 1 to 5, with 1 and 2 indicating that workers either received an adverse warning in their employment record (1) or a one- to two-day suspension (2). The highest estimates of 3–5 indicate a more aggressive punishment ranging from a three- to four-day unpaid suspension (3) to a five-day unpaid suspension (4) to a discharge (5).

Table 5.2 Infraction variations by average discipline score and division, 1984

	Divisions			
Infractions	*Emeryville (D2)*	*Richmond (D3)*	*East Oakland (D4)*	*Newark/ Hayward (D6)*
Failure to report	2	*	2.7	1
Controversy	2	*	5	*
Accident	3.7	2	3.8	0.3
Moving/license violations	*	*	2.5	*
Arriving to late or early	2	*	2.8	*
On sick book over 30 days	5	*	5	*
Insubordination	*	5	*	5
Excessive absenteeism	*	3.7	4	*
Failure to respond to supervisor inquiry	*	*	*	2
Fare box issues	*	*	*	1

$N=51$; standard deviation in parentheses. *No records of infractions for this offense during this period.

Source: Amalgamated Transit Union Local 192, Records: "Discipline Pending at Division Six, July 31, 1984"; "Memo to Edgar Jackson, Appeal Hearings, Wednesday, May 2, 1984"; "Memo to Edgar Jackson, Appeal Hearings, Wednesday, May 9, 1984"; "Memo to Edgar Jackson, Appeal Hearings, Wednesday, April 25, 1984"; "Memo to Edgar Jackson, Appeal Hearings, Wednesday, April 12, 1984"; "Memo to Edgar Jackson, Appeal Hearings, Wednesday, April 17, 1984."

Table 5.1 illustrates average differences in proposed discipline by division in 1984. Appeal hearing records support the observation made by operators that Division 4 drivers (D4, East Oakland) and Division 2 drivers (D2, Emeryville) suffered disproportionate punishment both in terms of frequency and severity. According to table 5.2, workers in D4 and D2, on average, suffered severe disciplinary action for infractions, while workers in Division 6 (D6, Newark/Hayward) received far less severe punishments for write ups.

Variations of infractions are staggering when we examine disparities in punishment for the same offense. As illustrated in table 5.2, it appears that AC Transit disciplined East Oakland and Emeryville (D4 and D2) drivers more severely than workers in Richmond and Newark/Hayward (D3 and D6). On the whole, two patterns emerge. Workers in D2 and D4 were written up for a variety of reasons, while workers in D2 and D6 were only cited for three to four types of infractions. A more intense pattern of surveillance existed in D2 and D4, primarily due to excessive absences and the district's attempt to crack down on workers arriving early or late at bus stops. The variation in punishment within and between divisions is not limited to the range of levied offenses but also reflects disparity in the level of punishments imposed for certain offenses.

Illustrated in table 5.2, D6 drivers who failed to report throughout 1984 primarily received adverse warnings in their files, while workers in D2 (Emeryville) and D4 (East Oakland) were suspended one to five days for their first failure to report an infraction. Meanwhile, workers in D6 also nearly escaped punishment for accidents, merely receiving adverse warnings, while accidents committed by D2 and D4 workers received heavy five-day or more suspensions without pay or discharge.

Drug Testing in the Transit Industry

In the mid-1980s and early 1990s, concerns about transit workers came to the fore, and the media framed drug and alcohol use in the industry as an epidemic. Railroad industry executive John R. Riley testified before the Senate Judiciary Committee, arguing that "substance abuse had invaded the railroad workplace." According to Riley, "A lawyer with a drinking problem may commit malpractice; a machinist using drugs could lose a finger. But a person operating a train under the influence of alcohol or drugs has a frightening ability to threaten the lives of fellow employees, passengers and any member of the public unfortunate to live near the site of a major accident. It's that difference in the degree to which public safety is placed in jeopardy that makes effective action so critical in our industry."[15] To back up his claim, he reported that between 1975 and 1984, drug and alcohol abuse contributed to at least forty-eight accidents, thirty-seven fatalities, eight nonfatal injuries, $20.4 million in railroad property damage, and $14 million in environmental cleanup. Citing the role substance abuse plays in the severity of accidents, Riley and others encouraged Congress to implement random drug testing in safety-sensitive positions.[16]

Opposition to random drug testing came from various individuals and organizations, including Gene Upshaw of the National Football League, R. V. Durham of the International Brotherhood of Teamsters, and Lawrence M. Mann, attorney of the Railway Labor Executives Association, who filed a lawsuit against the Federal Railroad Association on the basis that drug-testing rules were unconstitutional. Mann's baseline contention was that, while Riley's statistics were noteworthy, they failed to determine the extent to which accidents attributed to substance abuse were indeed caused by the substance. As Mann noted, "there are no recognized tests which will determine impairment ... [and] no threshold level ... that presents a serious problem."[17] According to Mann, Riley also failed to report the fact that all drug-testing procedures of the Civil Aeromedical Institute were currently under investigation following a guilty plea in May 1987 by its director, Dr. Delbert J. Lacefield, for falsifying three blood analysis reports the previous year. In 1987, Lacefield further conceded that he did not possess sufficient knowledge of blood plasma testing equipment used in the 1986 cases to accurately determine drug and alcohol levels. The 1986 cases involved in Lacefield's plea included a July 10 Union Pacific Railroad accident in Nebraska, an August 27 Conrail accident in Ohio, and a November 20 Santa Fe Railway accident in Mexico—each of which claimed lives and resulted in serious property damage. These cases are noteworthy because they ignited the crisis of control movement and, in particular, the national urge to implement random workplace drug testing.[18]

Additional problems threatened the integrity of efforts to drug test the workforce. R. V. Durham, director of safety and health for the International Brotherhood of Teamsters, recalled in his testimony before the Senate Judiciary Committee that "many of these employer-introduced programs do not adequately protect workers from having these programs administered in an arbitrary or discriminatory way."[19] Doctors such as John P. Morgan, MD, testified before the committee that "the application of screening tests in mass screening programs in the workplace has "generated more problems than [they] solve" because specialists had come to realize that screening tests were generally cheap and, because of their heightened sensitivity, possessed a high false positive rate.[20] In fact, Morgan reported that the Enzyme Immunoassay, EIA, test for the marijuana metabolite had been in wide use for six years before it was discovered that the test produced false positives in the presence of anti-inflammatory drugs such as ibuprofen.[21]

Despite claims by medical doctors like Dr. Morgan that drug testing in the workplace was an "expensive folly" and that the technology used to carry them out was "inadequate and misapplied," mass transportation firms throughout the country eventually implemented random drug tests.

In response, labor unions, including ATU 192, made various efforts through grievance arbitration procedures to protect workers from abuse by this bureaucratic intervention.

Before Random Substance Use Testing

The transportation industry has a long history of weeding out workers it suspects of abusing alcohol and drugs. The industry began substance abuse prevention well before the 1980s. Often with union support, since the early 1920s, transportation firms across the country developed informal programs to monitor employees believed to be suffering from chronic alcoholism. Although unions such as ATU and TWU did not fight humane efforts to deal with employees' drinking problems, they did challenge companies' adoption of programs that force employees to comply with the Alcoholics Anonymous method of rehabilitation because some employees preferred to seek assistance from qualified doctors or spiritual leaders. Unions also entertained concerns about efforts urging employees to join a substance abuse program, especially when the employee did not suffer a true addiction.

In 1953, White male driver E. E. Allen was the first employee to challenge Key System Transit's alcohol policy.[22] Allen admitted that he had consumed two glasses of wine less than three hours before going to work.[23] Arbitrator Arthur C. Miller ruled that, while Allen committed an infraction (alcohol had indeed been detected on his breath), his punishment should not be too harsh, considering his twenty-seven years of service to the district. Miller found there to be no convincing evidence that Allen was under the influence, besides the alcohol detected on his breath. Since this was a discharge case, Miller ruled that the district needed to provide "clear and convincing" evidence to support the case, not evidence that was "doubtful and speculative."[24]

In another case, this one involving White male driver Monroe Conley, Arbitrator Nevins chose not to sustain the recommended discharge because AC Transit's only evidence consisted of incongruent eyewitness testimony that differed on whether Conley had been intoxicated and smelled like alcohol at the scene of the accident.[25] Conley had chosen not to take the blood test, and Nevins found that his failure to take the test was not an admission of guilt, in turn ruling that the district must reinstate Conley. These early cases suggest some limits of AC Transit's pre-1980 substance control policy. However, as African American employment increased, the company became more stringent in its efforts to police its labor force.

In 1975, AC Transit and ATU 192 arbitrated a dispute regarding the discharge of Clawson Wallace, a new African American male transit operator who had been found driving under the influence of alcohol.[26] At approximately 8:20 P.M. on February 13, 1975, on the corner of Kittridge and Shattuck in downtown Berkeley, California, Wallace's supervisor discontinued his route and took him off his bus due to a complaint that he was off route and driving recklessly. During the arbitration, Wallace's supervisor testified that he received a call from central dispatch due to the complaints. Supervisor Lewis Scott, who had approached the bus, reported detecting a strong odor of alcohol on Wallace's breath. Scott also claimed that his eyes were red and that he had a "thick tongue" that prevented him from pronouncing his words properly.[27] Scott radioed to central dispatch and requested they send someone to validate his conclusions. After two supervisors verified the smell of alcohol on Wallace's breath, Superintendent Gauer asked Wallace to go to the hospital to take sobriety tests.

Wallace took deep offense to the request that he go to the hospital to take sobriety tests. At the arbitration, Gauer testified that Wallace adamantly refused to take the test, saying in response, "If the District would not take his word, they could have his badge." According to Gauer, Wallace further said that "he was a man and did not want to be treated like a boy." Upon his refusal to take the test, the district immediately suspended Wallace and directed him to return the next morning with the cold medicine and laxative that he claimed to be taking since he claimed to be suffering from an intense cold. However, when Wallace returned, he learned that AC Transit had discharged him.[28]

Due to the lack of hard evidence that Wallace was drinking, the union claimed he did not deserve to be discharged. Furthermore, the union emphatically argued that Wallace was a new driver suffering from a cold, that his normal speech was slow and sometimes slurred, and that his eyes were normally glassy and somewhat red. In the end, Wallace's grievance was denied because of his refusal to take the sobriety tests. Unlike in Monroe Conley's case, Wallace's refusal to take the test was interpreted as an admission of guilt.

AC Transit's termination of employees for failure to take the sobriety test was not the firm's only shift from previous practices. In the wake of Allen's 1953 case, cases involving operators admitting to consuming alcohol also ended in the favor of the district, as was the outcome for Paul J. Wilson. In these cases, the district strictly enforced an "under the slightest influence" standard, even when the only evidence was the odor of alcohol on an employee's breath. In 1975, Wilson reported to his supervisors that, having received some difficult news regarding a close family member, he had consumed an alcoholic beverage with lunch before reporting to work. In spite of Wilson's emotional struggles, the arbitrator ruled that his discharge was for just and sufficient cause. According to Arbitrator Barbara Bridgewater, the district had satisfied its obligation to establish that Wilson reported to work free from the slightest influence of alcohol.

This district's disparate application of the substance abuse policy is an example of its persistence in characterizing the actions of African American employees as insubordinate and incomprehensible. Several times over the years, the union attempted to clarify the definition of insubordination and limit the district's ability to sanction discipline solely on the basis of insubordination claims. Despite these efforts, we see, as in the case of Wallace, the company interpreting an African American's refusal to comply with a company sobriety test as subordination worthy of discharge. In Wallace's case, AC Transit made the decision to discharge the worker, and the arbitrator upheld and justified the firm's decision to force some workers to comply with alcohol testing, while in previous cases involving White men, discharge did not result from refusal to take a sobriety test.

ATU 192 Takes a Stand on Substance Abuse Policies,
Procedures, and Penalties

Records contained in the ATU 192's archives reveal that between the late 1970s and the late 1980s, over fourteen cases concerning discharges involving substance abuse were arbitrated. Throughout this period, ATU 192 masterfully refuted the findings of the laboratory AC Transit chose to conduct its drug and alcohol tests. ATU 192 also fiercely contested the district's policy regarding employees under the influence of intoxicants because the policy had not been negotiated with the union. The union did not disagree with the practice of pulling operators from service if reasonable suspicion existed and a properly executed investigation ensued. On the contrary, ATU 192 held that their biggest point of contention involved how AC Transit applied its policy and the extent to which the policy disproportionately hurt minority workers.

ATU 192 first made these arguments in October 1979 in an arbitration involving Berniece E. Johnson, an African American woman operator.[29] At approximately 9:25 A.M. on February 23 of that year, according to Dispatcher Thomas Ward's testimony, Ward had mentioned to Superintendent George E. Grandison that Johnson smelled of alcohol and that her speech was slurred.[30] Dispatchers Jack Patterson and O. B. Chadwick both corroborated Ward's observations. Patterson testified that he saw her just before Ward reported his suspicions to Superintendent Grandison and that when he approached her, she mumbled something he did not quite understand. He then approached Grandison and said he felt something was wrong with Johnson. When Chadwick came on duty, Grandison asked him to talk with Johnson. Chadwick approached Johnson in the Gilly Room, where transit operators congregate between shifts, and asked what was bothering her. When she told him she felt very sick, he could smell alcohol on her, according to his testimony. He also recalled that her eyes were red and that she was "pale and dry looking."[31]

According to Johnson, she was suffering from asthma and needed to use a variety of medications, including Sudafed, Hall's Mentholyptus Cough Drops, and Terpin Hydrate Cough Syrup. She also contended that she did not have anything to drink on February 23, 1978, and that the last time she had consumed alcohol was the on previous day when she had a shot of brandy and a beer during the day and a double shot of brandy before 9 P.M.[32] Since Grandison became aware of her alleged intoxication about 7 A.M., just before Johnson began her Montclair neighborhood route in San Francisco, he spoke with her for about ten minutes but did not smell alcohol on her breath. He testified that he followed up on these allegations again at 7:41 A.M., but still did not have a reason to suspect alcohol use. However, due to the suspicions of the other supervisors who claimed to smell alcohol on Johnson, Grandison asked her to take a blood test to address these concerns. She consented and went to Herrick Hospital for the test. The results of the blood tests indicated that Johnson's blood alcohol was .25 percent.[33] Based on the observations of her supervisors and the blood test results, the district argued that her discharge was valid and should be sustained because "enforcement of the alcohol rule cannot be tampered [with] in any way, for life and property are at stake."[34]

The AC Transit policy of pulling a driver from service when there is a reasonable suspicion that he or she has consumed alcohol dates to July 1, 1969. The union argued in the Johnson arbitration hearing that the district's policy of firing employees whose breath smelled of alcohol was not a well-established policy. In fact, ATU 192 argued that AC Transit had, in the past, reinstated drivers and workers in other classifications who were caught with alcohol on the job.[35] "It appears," they pointed out, "that a bus driver who sits and drinks alcohol on his bus may be reinstated, while a driver whose breath smells of a bit of drink he had before coming to work will not be reinstated. There is no basis in equity or in justice for such disparate treatment." Because AC Transit had charged Johnson with being under the influence of alcohol, ATU 192 argued that AC Transit violated her rights due to its failure to establish the level of intoxication that correlates with intoxication.[36]

During the arbitration, the union also pointed out that discharges in cases involving violations of drinking rules were often overturned when taking into consideration seniority and the "penalty should fit the crime doctrine." In the past, the district had reinstated workers on what it called a "non-precedent basis" so that these cases could not be used in arbitration hearings. In the Johnson arbitration, ATU 192 made attempts to reference previous cases, but these attempts were fruitless.[37]

The union further contended that the test administered to Johnson was tainted and should not have been used as a justification for discharging Johnson. ATU 192 argued that the lab test was a product of "speculation and hearsay" because of the inconsistencies in the testing process used by Herrick Hospital's lab and concerns regarding the credentials of the lab technicians who conducted the test. While ATU 192 considered the testing method used at Herrick Hospital appropriate for medical purposes, it did not meet the legal standard for forensic analysis.[38]

AC Transit claimed that the lab results did not need to meet the criminal standard of proof beyond a reasonable doubt. The district clarified that "an employer and employee do not stand in the relationship of prosecutor and defendant and that it is not accusing workers of criminal conduct." Rather a mere preponderance of the evidence, which included a .25 blood alcohol test in addition to observations from four witnesses who claimed to have detected the odor of alcohol and noticed signs that Johnson was under influence of alcohol, had compelled the district to discharge the employee. AC Transit also contended that all discrimination claims were "unsupported by any reliable evidence" and were not only "implausible" but "outrageous."[39]

ATU 192 argued that using misinterpreted results to discharge an employee was itself a crime, and it contended that the district failed to acknowledge errors in the testing procedure, potentially corrupting the results of the blood test conducted at Herrick Hospital. First, the union maintained that Herrick Hospital's use of alcohol swabs to sanitize the arm prior to the blood alcohol test contaminated the sample. Second, it argued that the head of the lab, Mary Joyce, was not qualified to run the equipment because she did not understand the procedure, what solution or enzyme should serve as a buffer in the test, or how to interpret test results.

ATU 192 further argued that Herrick was not a licensed forensic blood alcohol lab and that its equipment was not set up or calibrated by the State Department of Health. Since Herrick's procedures did not require the technician to provide at least five tests—a negative control, a positive control, a quality control unknown, and two patient samples—Herrick lab's procedures, according to ATU 192, did not meet the quality and accuracy control standards established by Title 17 of the California Administrative Code.

According to ATU 192, AC Transit could have avoided violating Title 17 standards by paying $35 to have Johnson tested at the Institute of Forensic Sciences in Oakland. Concluding that a blood alcohol rate beyond .15 is extremely high, the union contended that the reported level of .25 percent extends beyond the level at which most people would be extremely intoxicated. But, since Johnson was able to drive her early morning route and pass field sobriety tests by not exhibiting mental slowness and difficulties with walking and talking, AC Transit erred in using this test to support its conclusions.

ATU 192 presented many theories to support its contention that AC Transit was trying to find a way to terminate Johnson. ATU 192 claimed AC Transit management may have had an axe to grind because Johnson, who was hired pursuant to the settlement of a sex discrimination lawsuit, had submitted an application for promotion. The union also contended that AC Transit violated Johnson's due process rights by failing to provide the witness statements of Chadwick, Ward, and Patterson to Johnson or the union prior to the arbitration hearing so that these parties might secure a rebuttal witness. Finally, ATU 192 maintained that AC Transit actively prevented the blood sample from being cross-examined because the sample was not preserved after Herrick conducted its tests.[40]

In response to ATU 192's arguments, Arbitrator Geraldine M. Randall concluded there was no evidence AC Transit destroyed the blood sample in bad faith. In addition, the district did not actually destroy the supporting evidence; instead, she contended that the neutral party, Herrick Hospital, destroyed the sample so ATU 192 could not argue that the district orchestrated these events to undermine Johnson's case. With regard to the union's assertion that AC Transit withheld witness statements, Randall argued there was no evidence that AC Transit breached their contract by withholding evidence requested during the grievance process. Randall also noted that there was no evidence the union had even initiated the discovery mechanisms included in their contract.

While Randall acknowledged that the blood tests may be "off by a significant percentage," she maintained that the test result was correct to indicate that a problem existed. She went on to argue "The test could be in error, for whatever reasons, by as much as 150 percent without affecting a conclusion that [the] Grievant was presumably under the influence of alcohol in the criminal sense." Based on the observations of the district's witnesses alone, Randall contended that the district had proven its decision to discharge Johnson was correct. Randall argued that based on previous arbitration awards, including Tennessee River Pulp and Paper Co, 68 LA 421; Union Pacific Railroad Co, 44 LA 772, 773; and Cal Custom Hawk, 65 LA 723, 727, expert testimony is not required to prove intoxication. According to Randall, AC Transit simply needed to offer a preponderance of evidence capable of convincing "a reasonable person" that Johnson violated the alcohol rule. Also according to Randall, AC Transit did not have to prove that Johnson was under the influence according to a criminal standard, given that the district has a duty to provide safe service to their patrons. As such, Randall found that AC Transit's alcohol rule was "justifiable in public transportation, though it might be found too severe in other contexts." So, despite the fact that the arbitrator considered the union's arguments about the blood test to be "masterful," in the end, they were irrelevant because Randall perceived that "the test [did] not make the District's case; it merely enhance[d] it."[41]

On August 1, 1979, a few months prior to Randall's decision, Personnel Analyst Wayne Onizuka wrote to Richard K. Windrich, the then president of ATU 192, to inform him that the district had decided to have the Institute of Forensic Sciences Western Laboratories in Oakland conduct all blood and urine tests of suspected employees. He also confirmed that duplicate samples would be made available for independent testing. Onizuka concluded that the district's choice to utilize the Title 17 procedure "in no way is an admission that criminal standards apply in any fashion to the discipline procedures between the District and the union."[42]

By December 27, 1989, when ATU 192 attempted to advocate for Margaret Hayes, a service worker in the Maintenance Department at the Emeryville Division on December 27, 1989, most defensive attempts against AC Transit's substance use policy and its implementation had proven unsuccessful.[43] So this time, ATU 192 embraced a new strategy: to argue that the district did not establish a reasonable cause for testing Hayes, who was placed on paid administrative leave pending the outcome of the test. On August 8, Hayes had been suspended pending discharge for violating AC Transit's rules regarding substance use while on duty. Her blood test came back positive, revealing that she had a substantial amount of cocaine in her system (.89 micrograms), and she was discharged following a hearing on October 14, 1988.[44]

This downward spiral began for Hayes upon return from her grandfather's funeral, when, on July 26, 1988, the head of the Maintenance Department in Emeryville, Anthony Haile, paged her to his office and requested that she submit verification of attendance at the funeral. During the meeting, Superintendent Haile began to suspect that Hayes was under the influence of a substance because "she was acting nervous and was just running off at the mouth talking." Although she claimed to be sick and taking medication for her blood pressure, Haile said he "figured she was on something else" and asked her to take a blood test to prove that she was not under the influence of drugs. After leaving the room to find a supervisor in order to collaborate his suspicions as per district, Hayes quickly changed her clothes, clocked out, told a supervisor that she was sick, and began to head home. Haile tried to compel her back to work with the threat of discharging her for insubordination, but Hayes ignored him—that is, until Haile caught up with her on 45th Avenue, and as he recalled, "grabbed her arm, and physically pulled her back onto Division property." Soon she found herself back at work.[45]

ATU 192 tried to argue that "the issue in this case is not whether there was a high level or a small level of cocaine" in Hayes' system,[46] but rather that the issue at hand was AC Transit's failure to comply with Hayes's civil and due process rights because it did not establish reasonable cause to compel her to take the test. The union also argued that employees should not be tested unless the district can demonstrate that it has secured objective evidence to support the suspicion of substance use. AC Transit contested this argument, maintaining that reasonable cause to test had indeed been secured once Haile's assumption about Hayes found support in Chuck Lacy, another AC Transit supervisor. In the end, according to AC Transit, the blood test revealed the truth about Hayes's condition by proving that the many excuses she used to justify the various symptoms observed by the supervisors were "just that: excuses."

Arbitrator Charles L. Askin sided with AC Transit in his finding that Hayes's discharge was for just and sufficient cause. Although the union requested that she return to work upon successful completion of a drug treatment program, Askin contended that the "unfortunate traumas in her personal life" cannot be viewed as mitigating factors. According to Askin, "Having unfortunate personal problems, while possibly explaining her conduct in this case, does not provide a basis for reversing this discharge in view of the district's duty of care and its consistent policy of terminating employees who violate its drug and alcohol rules."[47] Before the adopting of federally mandated drug-testing policies, AC Transit had unevenly and inequitable instituted its substance abuse policies, regularly disadvantaging African American workers, both men and women. However, even when ATU 192 worked to defend workers facing termination for substance abuse policy violations, these efforts were typically unsuccessful. In the end, both ATU 192 and the workers knew that AC Transit's substance abuse testing policy—and the policy's various problems were here to stay.

Federally Mandated Drug Testing Comes to AC Transit

Although ATU 192 continued to dispute AC Transit's substance abuse policies, its efforts diminished considerably during the 1990s due to several factors. One reason for the decline is that attempts to challenge the company's substance abuse policies were unsuccessful. Another factor was the indisputability of cases involving crack-cocaine and marijuana, two substances which had gained a reputation as "public enemy number one."

After the Urban Mass Transportation Administration issued regulations in December 1988 requiring all local transit systems receiving federal funds to test employees for drug use—and not only on the occasion of suspicions, but randomly as well—the U.S. District Court of Appeals for the District of Columbia claimed that the agency was acting beyond its congressionally mandated authority in imposing nationwide drug-testing rules on local transit agencies. This decision in favor of transport unions reversed an earlier decision by the U.S. District Court. TWU and the ATU had contended that the Urban Mass Transportation Administration did not have the authority to impose the federal drug-testing program. The new regulations required local transit authorities to utilize urinalysis testing before employment, after an accident, when an employee is suspected to be intoxicated, and at random.

In addition to the Federal Appeal Court's opinion, California State Court judges temporally postponed random drug testing for AC Transit and Muni as well as the San Mateo County Transit District. But as the courts began to allow testing under certain circumstances, unions and transit firms alike began to prepare for what they anticipated was ahead. According to the media, transit officials feared that as many as one-fifth of the nearly 10,000 Bay Area transit workers would not pass the drug tests. As a result, transit officials started planning for the possibility of having to replace workers who flunked the test or outright refused to take it.[48]

Donna Hemmilia, a *San Francisco Business Times* staff writer, reported on January 6, 1990, that AC Transit workers were the first in the country to successfully halt federally mandated random testing with a preliminary injunction ordered by Alameda County Superior Court Judge Michael Ballachey. Workers contended that these random tests violated their right to privacy under the state constitution. They were also concerned that the test results might be inaccurate and could be used to fire innocent workers. Judge Ballachey determined that the drug-testing laws proposed by the Urban Mass Transportation Administration violated workers' right to privacy. In addition, he ruled that the district did not provide sufficient evidence to prove a need for random drug testing. So he barred the planned testing pending a full trial on the issue.

The California State Superior Court eventually ruled that the federal drug-testing plans did not violate California's constitutional ban on unreasonable government searches since the workers subject to the law held sensitive positions. Due in large part to public pressure to "get tough" on drug abusers, policymakers first passed the law to authorize random drug testing in 1989. The final drug-testing rules established in 1989 required federally funded firms employing safety-sensitive employees to test at random for marijuana, cocaine, amphetamines, opiates, and phencyclidine.[49]

Transit employers were generally supportive of the drug-testing regulations. Transportation employers claimed that since 1975, damages caused by employees who were impaired by alcohol and other drugs caused thirty-seven deaths and eight injuries, in addition to nearly $34 billion in property damage.[50] Before the law's implementation, L. A. Kimball, chair of the American Public Transportation Association Drug and Alcohol Abuse Task Force, commended federal efforts to "take action on this constant, growing threat to our national transportation network" and only complained that the deadline for the implementation of these drug-testing programs was too short.[51] Later, in 1991, Congress adopted a bill that reauthorized random drug testing of safety-sensitive workers and added alcohol to the list of drugs to test.[52]

In my interviews, I found that transit operators also seemed to accept random drug testing. In fact, many at AC Transit described random drug testing as a needed and appropriate intervention in their line of work. They recalled that they did not much mind being pulled from the schedule to take a random drug test because they would get three hours from the time of the notice to take the test. However, these workers also repeatedly mentioned a concern that random drug testing was not very random, especially at the beginning. Most AC Transit operators were certain that African Americans were being subjected to random drug testing more often than other workers. Katherine, an AC Transit operating of twenty-one years, was particularly bothered by what she and many of her colleagues referred to as being singled out. As she recalled, "I felt like it was unfair when it first started. It seemed like I was being drug tested, almost every month. They were pulling me, and somebody told me after 10 years they really start picking with you to try to get you out. It seems like every month they were drug testing me, and I noticed that it was a lot of old timers that had never been drug tested and the drug testing had been going on for about two years. The thing they had told us was that it was random and that the computer picked out whomever. But, it was full of the same people all of the time."

Katherine was not the only person who observed the company disproportionately testing African Americans and who suspected something was wrong with their selection method. Like Katherine, Georgia also thought that AC Transit was targeting people they wanted to have leave the company before retirement. When I asked her how this practice this could be possible, she said she was not sure. "But," she said, "it is clear that everybody's not being tested. It's supposed to be random, but when you go to the testing facilities, you see nothing but Black faces."

Meanwhile, there was another disturbing pattern at work. Even those who supported drug testing and the employment assistance programs designed to help those caught with drugs in their system to get their lives back on track mentioned that this employment practice seemed to play a significant role in the termination of African American supervisors. In fact, Ruth explained that "most of the people that are gone due to drug testing had high seniority and were Black. There are some White people that have never been tested."

Ruth is very familiar with the testing facilities because over the course of five years, she spent a great deal of time there due to the discovery of prescription drugs in her system. As she recalled, "If you are caught positive in that random drug testing, which I was, they will test you anytime, day or night, that you are on their property to see if you are still using drugs or not." Ruth told me that she was not on street drugs and that she was taking a medication that she didn't report to AC Transit "But it was considered drugs anyway," she recalled, despite the fact that the testing doctor who identified the drug in her system said that he did not think she was using the prescription recreationally. Ruth claimed that the woman running the drug-testing program for AC Transit, overruled the doctor, but Ruth did not give up without a fight.

I fought it, and fought it. But, I had to go into a program and I was only there 14 days. When I got back to work, for five years, I was on that program, and I must have been tested a hundred times. . . . The union was not experienced or advanced or anything. I actually went outside and got a few lawyers. Each one of them within the year declined my case after they took my money. So, I tried to fight it . . . then I said, I can't fight it. You can't fight them all. But, they did me wrong. How many other people got caught up like this?

A Look Inside AC Transit's Random
Drug and Alcohol Testing Program

The FTA audited AC Transit's drug and alcohol testing program, and the records reveal that the company consistently and pervasively deviated from federal policy and abused its power. FTA Substance Abuse Management Oversight Audit Reports from 1998 to 2010 demonstrate AC Transit's difficulties with developing a random drug and alcohol testing program in addition to their difficulty creating a properly staffed Substance Abuse Program drawing on qualified substance abuse professionals. According to these reports, FTA regulators expressed a variety of concerns regarding the deficiencies in AC Transit's alcohol/substance abuse procedures and guidelines as well as its record management not to mention the company's problems with breath alcohol collections. Federal auditors admonished AC Transit for not developing an effective urine collection procedure and not ensuring a genuinely random selection of employees for testing.

In 1998, the federal government cited AC Transit's management procedures for deviations from policy that included not listing a contact person to answer employee questions about the substance abuse testing program and not providing the workforce with a list of the employee categories subject to testing as required by the antidrug and alcohol prevention program. AC Transit had been subjecting non-safety-sensitive employees to testing, and, following audits, the FTA forced the company to inform employees that only safety-sensitive workers are required by federal law to take drug tests and that testing non-safety-sensitive workers is not federal policy, but rather company policy.[53]

By the October 1998 audit, transit districts were required to prohibit substance abuse not only under the Drug Free Workplace Act of 1988 but also under the alcohol misuse prevention portion of the FTA Rule Requirement specified in section 654.71(b)(4).[54] However, AC Transit did not identify alcohol as a prohibitive substance or specify times of required compliance with the alcohol misuse prevention rule or the consequences of a failed alcohol test. While AC Transit did prohibit drug abuse, the FTA cited the transit district for not specifying the drugs it prohibited and for its lack of clarity in specifying the circumstances under which it would test employees, especially with reference to random testing and return-to-duty testing. Additionally, the FTA cited AC Transit in 1999 for not issuing a discussion of procedures used to test for prohibited drugs or procedures used to preserve the integrity and validity of the drug-testing process.[55]

When FTA audited the program in 1998, they also noticed that AC Transit failed to clearly state from where it derived the right to impose testing—whether from the FTA or an independent authority. In several instances, especially those involving AC Transit's explanation of testing mandates and rules regarding prohibited amounts, AC Transit tended to inaccurately characterize their efforts as FTA mandates. AC Transit policy also inaccurately stated that "identifiable traces of a prohibited substance" are subject to discipline or discharge under FTA mandate. On the contrary, FTA auditors corrected AC Transit by stating that the "FTA mandates specific amounts, not detectable traces."[56]

Furthermore, the 1998 FTA audit uncovered that the medical review officer, Terrance S. McGee, MD, failed to interview employees with positive laboratory tests in order to determine whether the results were indicative of legal or prohibited substance usage, as mandated by the FTA—or, in the event of a positive test, first attempt to contact the employee regarding the confirmed test result.[57] Instead, according to the 1999 audit, it is clear that the medical review officer regularly contacted the employer first, instead of first requesting that the employee contact him to discuss the test. By McGee's admission, he advised the employer to pull the driver off the road without first discussing the results with the employee on a confidential basis.[58] In addition, AC Transit failed to inform employees that they had seventy-two hours to request a split specimen for independent testing and to contract with a Department of Health and Human Services–certified laboratory for urine analysis services.[59]

Apparently, based on the 1998 audit, AC Transit also failed to hire a substance abuse counselor with the credentials of a substance abuse professional (SAP). The FTA acknowledged that John R. Schlim, who was the AC Transit SAP, had an impressive resume; however, despite his extensive experience, the FTA noted that he did not meet the qualifications of a SAP under the FTA program because he was not a medical doctor and did not possess the required specialized knowledge and clinical experience in diagnosing and treating individuals with substance abuse issues.[60]

Furthermore, AC Transit struggled with the persistent problem of making sure all employees selected for random testing actually took the test. In the first quarter of 1997, only one out of six employees selected for a random test took the test, and throughout this year, less than half the workers selected for random testing actually complied. The same year, AC Transit also failed to document the reasons for excusal from random testing, as cited by the audit.[61]

When, in December 1999, the FTA conducted a follow-up to the 1998 audit of AC Transit's drug-testing program, it found that the transit district was still falling short of following federal law. For instance, AC Transit was not testing late-night and early morning employees on the graveyard shift, which represented a failure to conform to the FTA's new policy of requiring random tests around the clock and on all days and hours among the safety-sensitive workforce.[62] Furthermore, AC Transit continued to have a high incidence of "shy bladder," which enabled some employees to evade testing. FTA rules state that employees can only be excused for legitimate reasons, including long-term disability, maternity leave, extended vacation, and worker's comp—not shy bladder. Finally, despite the significant number of excusals, auditors found that AC Transit still failed to record its reasons for excusal from random testing.[63]

As we can see in table 5.3, which provides the percentage of workers excused from random drug and alcohol testing in 1997, 1998, and 2000, AC Transit's tendency to allow some workers to avoid testing improved over time. In 1997, 70 percent of workers selected for testing were excused, but by 2000, 40 percent of workers selected for testing were excused.

The FTA's 2002 audit of AC Transit's random testing problem noted that the firm still was struggling to implement the required standards. In this audit, the FTA discovered that AC Transit's contractor also made various mistakes in completing custody forms and performing alcohol and drug testing. For instance, auditors found that during this year, nearly one-third of the tests for drugs and alcohol were not performed properly. The FTA required AC Transit to correct these errors and inform the agency of the methods used in order to correct these findings.[64]

Lastly, The FTA found AC Transit was failing to comply with its test rate rules. The FTA requires that transit districts complete tests equivalent to 50 percent of safety-sensitive employees for drug testing and 10 percent of these employees for alcohol testing. However, the FTA noticed that AC Transit was "seriously out of compliance" in meeting the requirements of testing 50 percent of the covered employees for drug testing, and, in addition, AC Transit failed to ensure that its contractor, Friendly Transportation, was drawing an adequate random selection on a monthly basis and completing both urine and breath collections in a timely matter. What is more, the FTA cited AC Transit for failing to conduct random drug and alcohol tests during weekends in 1999 and before

Table 5.3 Workers excused from random drug and alcohol testing in 1997, 1998, and 2000–2001

	Year		
Type of Substance Abuse Test	*1997*	*1998*	*2000–2001*
Urine	20	48	32
Both	10	15	17
Percentage excused	70	38	40

Source: Federal Transit Administration, "Drug and Alcohol Testing Results that AC Transit Reported to FTA," for Years 1997, 1998, 2000–2001, 2003, 2005, 2007, and 2009, Pursuant to FOIA Request to U.S. Department of Transportation, Federal Transit Administration, file no. 10-0106.

or after the period of 12:05 P.M. to 2:15 P.M. during weekdays throughout the third quarter of 1999.[65]

As we can see in table 5.4, while nearly reaching the required percentage of random tests among drivers in 2003, AC Transit began testing fewer drivers between 2005 and 2009. In 2005, the company tested 53 percent of its drivers, while, in 2009, it only tested 26 percent of its drivers. Meanwhile, as the transit operators outlined in their interviews, AC Transit directed its drug-testing efforts toward supervisors and dispatchers, especially between 2003 and 2007. Until 2009, supervisors and dispatchers were more likely to submit to alcohol testing than drivers. For instance, in 2003, 19 percent of supervisors and dispatchers took alcohol tests, while only 9 percent of drivers found themselves subject to these tests. By 2007, 4 percent of drivers took alcohol tests compared to 12 percent of supervisors and dispatchers.

Summary

Working on the premise that bus accidents and service delays are largely due to distracted or lazy workers, transit employers such as AC Transit have been known to establish bureaucratic rules that harshly penalize and discipline workers for engaging in unproductive behavior. In turn, frustrations voiced by transit operators throughout the country regarding patterns of strict discipline echo in the ranks of workers caught up in AC Transit's efforts to monitor workers' behavior and punish those who have violated company policies. This chapter documents patterns of dis-

Table 5.4 Percentage of random drug and alcohol testing participation by job title and year, 2003–2009

	2003		2005		2007		2009	
Type of Test	Drivers	Supervisors/ Dispatchers	Drivers	Supervisors/ Dispatchers	Drivers	Supervisors/ Dispatchers	Drivers	Supervisors/ Dispatchers
Drug testing	46	81	53	41	30	55	26	16
Alcohol testing	9	19	18	19	4	12	10	4

Source: Federal Transit Administration, "Drug and Alcohol Testing Results that AC Transit Reported to FTA," for Years 1997, 1998, 2000–2001, 2003, 2005, 2007, and 2009, Pursuant to FOIA Request to U.S. Department of Transportation, Federal Transit Administration, file no. 10-0106.

cipline among AC Transit operators for infractions ranging from miss-outs to using the bathroom without permission and not having both hands on the steering wheel despite the fact that devices needed to operate the buses are not all located on this wheel. While contending with a "plantation style of management," workers are expected to labor under harsh conditions and are constantly forced to sacrifice their well-being and safety under the continual threat of job loss.

Like many other worker-centered reforms designed to improve productivity and ensure public safety, AC Transit's efforts to address substance abuse among transit workers have been questionable for quite some time. Since 1975, well before federally mandated drug testing emerged, AC Transit began severely punishing workers for substance use violations. ATU 192 challenged AC Transit's inconsistent company policies regarding alcohol testing, but, despite these efforts, AC Transit continued to disproportionately apply alcohol testing and penalties for abuse. In addition, arbitrators involved in disputes about these polices have supported the district's decision to allow White male employees admitting to the consumption of alcohol to keep their job, while typically discharging Black employees for the same offense.

Beyond the blatant inconsistency in applying its substance abuse policies, AC Transit also violated a variety of FTA rules governing its drug-testing program. The federal government's drug-testing program requires firms to be specific about the drugs they prohibit and to specify the circumstances under which they test workers. AC Transit failed to develop a drug-testing program that randomly screened all workers. Rather, the district specifically targeted employees who worked certain shifts and on certain days, enabling some workers to refuse to take the test without penalty.

AC Transit's drug surveillance lacked integrity because it failed to honor the federal guidelines designed to help ensure fairness in the drug-testing program and prevent discrimination. The list of AC Transit's infractions is substantial: the company did not set parameters for each substance, terminated workers under the slightest influence, failed to provide samples to workers for individual testing, avoided informing workers of dirty tests, and hired an unqualified doctor to lead its drug assistance program.

On top of these failures, AC Transit also neglected to implement an effective record management system or develop a mandated program designed to monitor alcohol abuse among all safety-sensitive workers. Although absenteeism, accidents, diminished productivity, and other work-related problems have consistently been associated with alcohol abuse, AC Transit treated alcohol abuse in a less punitive manner than drug use—and was not alone in this approach. Research from the American Management Association confirms the selective nature of random drug testing, especially when this testing became popular in the early to mid-1990s. According to the American Management Association, employers, who are free to select the substances they would like to test for, are much more likely to test for illegal drugs than to test for alcohol. In the communications, utilities, and transportation industries in particular, data from 1992–1993 reveal that while 72 percent of these firms tested for drug abuse, only 35 percent also tested for alcohol abuse.[66] In turn, employers have responded very differently to employees with alcohol in their system than to employees whose testing shows positive for illegal drugs. For instance, many companies have developed employee assistance programs to address alcohol abuse, while companies typically respond to drug use with formal penalties ranging from denial of employment to suspensions and terminations—and this, despite lingering concerns regarding the capability of drug-testing efforts to deal adequately with risk of impairment.

These disparities emerged as the drug abuse crisis began to mount, and transit firms, like many other employers in the business community, tended to oversimplify the problem and its causes. Many employers have been quick to point out that alcohol is legal. At the same time, employers saw drug use in the form of crack-cocaine or meth addiction as largely "a problem of poverty" and believed it did not share the legal and social acceptance of alcohol. As a result, companies perceived illegal drug abuse as a threat to people and most of all, to profit. In fact, given its association with the HIV infection, illegal drug use became the official focus of management's crisis of control movement. Support for drug testing in the workplace also came from top-ranking leaders of the federal government. While funding for drug treatment declined by 25 percent during the Reagan administration, former President Clinton continued to support the Reagan and George H. W. Bush administrations' initiatives by promoting the virtues of drug-testing programs and increasing funding for law enforcement efforts to address this problem.[67]

Many unions, legal scholars, and medical professionals have challenged the usefulness of drug testing because of its disproportionate implementation in the service sector industries as well as because of the technological limitations in the primary method of testing for drug use during the period of study, the Enzyme Multiplied Immunoassay Test (EMIT). Recently, studies have emerged documenting that these tests produce false positives for marijuana. There is also some concern that drug testing using EMIT can be racially biased because individuals with a higher melanin content in their skin are more likely to produce a false positive. Given this degree of inaccuracy, several district courts have rejected the sole use of EMIT tests as the means of establishing drug use. Despite concerns about the quality of this urinalysis test, firms have substantially increased their use of these tests, which are the cheapest, most easily administered, and least intrusive among the various drug-testing methods.[68]

While drug testing is fraught with questions surrounding its accuracy and its ability to measure impairedness, this bureaucratic innovation has, in effect, granted firms control over workers' behavior both on and off the job. While attendance policies enable employers such as AC Transit to coerce employees into working despite circumstances such as illness and fatigue that would prompt them to call in sick from work, drug-testing programs go a step further by increasing employers' power over workers and the capacity to oversee their personal lives. Random drug and alcohol testing extends the scope of the employer's control over the worker from the workplace to the worker's personal spaces. While off the job, those who use illegal and legal substances to deal with stress, fatigue, or, in some cases pain stand the chance of losing their job if traces of these substances are found in their system.

Although some would argue that transit operators caught with drugs and/or alcohol should be punished because they may be placing members of the public in harm's way, it is a well-known fact that recreational substance use is a maladaptive response to stress, especially among low-skilled employees engaged in repetitive and dangerous work. Countless studies have associated cigarette smoking, drinking, and prescription pill abuse to being overworked and stress. Instead of minimizing the stress, drug-testing efforts and other methods designed to control and monitor workers, particularly in firms such as AC Transit, have exacerbated the oppressive and stress-laden conditions within the workplace. Similar to the more recent invasion of employee privacy in the form of phone, internet, and email surveillance, drug testing and other administrative means used to micromanage workers represent a punitive turn in the culture of opportunity, especially when a company implements these reforms that disproportionately impact the newest cohorts of workers.

While it has been said that certain very large corporations are "too big to fail," evidence from this study suggests that workers are often set up to fail. In the wrong hands, worker-centered reforms, including drug testing, attendance policies, uniform regulations, parking enforcement efforts, and more are, at base, arbitrary methods of social closure that profoundly shape the structure of opportunity available to workers. By adopting rules and practices of worker surveillance, employers invoke company standards and public safety claims to justify a waning commitment to good labor conditions. At the same time, they seek to persuade workers "caught" in these surveillance mechanisms that reprisals are a consequence of personal failure and that the choices they have made (to skip work, to take medications, to use alcohol, for example) are inherently personal and do not stem from demanding work conditions. Ultimately, these worker-centered reforms function as modern forms of Jim Crow–era deference rituals that appear neutral on the surface but, when employed by a resistant organization, may become a blatantly defensive and oppressive means to undermine and underutilize workers deemed undeserving.

In this chapter, I have traced the evolution of drug testing and the consequences of other strategies of surveillance within AC Transit. I have also chronicled ATU 192's responses to disciplinary patterns. In the next chapter, I conclude this discussion by engaging the implications of my findings, especially with regard to punishment disparities and the ways declining working conditions observed within low-skilled workplaces shape the structure of opportunity available to workers like the African American women operators featured in this study. These women workers, similar to many other low-skilled workers, have surpassed previous generations in gaining access to once coveted positions from which they were historically excluded. However, after securing these jobs, many of them soon discovered that the benefits were not what they used to be.

6

A House Divided

The Impact of Persistent Bias on Low-Skilled Workers

This extended case study demonstrates the degree to which institutional efforts have influenced the employment circumstances and opportunities available to African American women and other similarly situated workers. Evidence in this study illustrates that prior to 1978, AC Transit thrived economically, funded in significant part by a reliance on property taxes in addition to state and federal money. With these resources and a growing ridership, AC Transit rose from the ashes of a collapsed transportation company to become one of the nation's model transit systems. AC Transit was forced to address complaints of job discrimination due to its refusal to hire African American women as transit operators in 1974. In this study, I document how the culture of opportunity transformed from one in which inequality within AC Transit was maintained through savage and visible forms of exclusion based on race-based antagonisms and gender norms, to a more subtle savagery that justifies exclusion on the basis of perceived characteristics of a population that are well supported by dominant cultural narratives and stereotypes.

Although AC Transit eventually altered its hiring process to the point of significantly decreasing the number of White and male new hires, the firm's changes to the labor process and its disproportionate implementation of arbitrary workplace rules constitute evidence of AC Transit's symbolic compliance with its own affirmative action plan. When confronted with the need to change its hiring procedures, AC Transit made secondary adjustments that included placing new demands on workers and restructuring the labor process in ways that drastically altered the culture of opportunity available to workers. Evidence further illustrates that this firm implemented personnel policies as well as upper level managerial decisions that were disproportionately applied. While restructuring human resource policies and ignoring arbitration hearing decisions contrary to their new management strategies, AC Transit demonstrated an increasing tendency to neglect its obligation to protect its workers from occupational hazards that include faulty equipment and stress caused by rude or dangerous patrons. Once the buses began to include state-of-the-art surveillance equipment and the firm started to employ random drug testing, AC Transit operators did not just feel as though they had lost control of their work lives, they also began to feel as though their personal lives were also being consumed by work rules and pressures.

Understanding the Workplace Integration in the Post–Affirmative Action Era

From Barbara Reskin and Patricia Roos, we learn that when women entered nontraditional jobs during the 1970s and 1980s, these workplaces transformed in significant ways. Rather than creating wage parity and expanding access to managerial positions, firms tended to concentrate women workers in jobs that were increasingly deskilled or in positions with limited mobility and earning potential. According to Reskin and Roos's theory of gender labor valuation, these jobs declined in quality once the demographic composition of the workplace began to increasingly represent women workers, who are lower ranked in the labor queue than the men they replaced.

Just as the increase of women workers in an occupation promotes steady declines in job quality, especially with regard to pay and promotion opportunities, demographic shifts in the racial composition of the workplace also generate changes in the work opportunity available to workers. Marlese Durr and John Logan establish the existence of "minority submarkets" in 1991 by interviewing seventy-nine highly educated African Americans employed by New York State and pointing out that while these wages appear comparable to those of African Americans in similar mainstream jobs, there is less civil service job protection and fewer or no higher management positions available to them. These researchers find limited mobility between submarkets because it is harder to transition to a mainstream job from a minority submarket job than to transition from a minority submarket job to the mainstream. Similarly, scholars like Evelyn Nakano Glenn have analyzed the work challenges of women of color by viewing their employment options as a product of their relational power in American society. In *Unequal Freedom*, Glenn contends that women of color are undermined by exclusion practices, which are influenced by racial and gender norms that impact how tasks are determined, how job categories are created, and the extent to which the coercive labor policies and practices that emerged limited opportunity and worker autonomy in the workplace.[1]

By documenting African American women's journey as transit workers within AC Transit, this study contributes to existing theories of workplace inequality by helping to lay the groundwork for the development and application of an inclusive theory of workplace integration. This theory of workplace integration takes into account the various internal and external pushes and pulls that shape the structure of opportunity available to workers who occupy different status positions within desegregating occupations. It functions to help theorize about the factors that limit and constrain the structure of opportunity and its cultural legitimation within firms.

This theory emerged as I considered the reasons employment insecurity and immobility emerged within AC Transit as well as the broader implications of the findings in this case study. I noticed that upon hire, workers are assigned to one of three distinctive paths that assist in determining their level of success within a firm which include the paths of the chosen, the gap-fillers, and the tightrope walkers. African American women workers' association with or placement on a path within this desegregating workplace reflected their positioning within the labor queue, which is shaped by the nature of race- and gender-based antagonisms among similarly situated workers as well as management. Within unionized occupations like transit operating, the chosen may find their working conditions imperfect. However, they are likely to possess the capacity to influence changes within the workplace and reap the benefits of these changes because their access to upward mobility and employment security is not heavily contested by coworkers and management. Gap-fillers are treated like strikebreakers who only gain access to jobs on the cusp of decline that are responding to significant labor shortages. The needs of gap-fillers are often ignored because they gained access to the occupation when the employer was desperate for help. Their chances of securing workplace improvements are shaped by the extent to which these workers are concentrated within particular departments or positions within the firm as well as their level of acceptance among colleagues, their union, as well as management. Meanwhile, tightrope walkers secure coveted positions when they are in decline. For them, the declining coveted position is an upgrade from their previous employment placements; however, the structure of opportunity available to them will differ substantially from the workplace opportunity available to those on the chosen path in part due to the level of mistrust their presence motivates among coworkers and management as well as the collectively held assumption that they are unfit to labor. Like gap-fillers, they may come to convince fellow workers that they have a legitimate claim to the job; however, by the time tightrope walkers gain access to the coveted job, it has become highly deferential and punitive in nature. In addition, workers' access to occupational rewards may continue to be limited by methods of social closure employed by the union as well as management.

As a result, tightrope walkers, like the African American women transit operators featured in this analysis, encounter difficulties oftentimes as soon as they gain access to the occupation. They are typically singled out and among the first to be "dissed" and dismissed on the job. When frustrations with physical injury and stress mount and these workers push back, they are often put in their prescribed place and shown the door.

Various factors contributed to AC Transit's and ATU 192's lack of responsiveness to the concerns about physical injury and stress voiced by African American women and similarly situated workers. It is likely that both AC Transit management's and ATU 192's core belief that driving is "men's work" prompted them to ignore complaints of injury and stress because these problems, from their perspective, proved that women were not fit to hold the position. As noted in chapter 3, bias against women was a widespread problem within the transit industry, especially in the East Bay area. I did not uncover any evidence that AC Transit made attempts to accommodate the physical and personal needs of these workers until the company was forced to acknowledge their concerns. Furthermore, since the late 1980s, ATU 192 leaders primarily consisted of African American men. While these leaders seemed more in touch with the negative consequences of the new work rules that emerged soon after African American women began working for AC Transit in large numbers, evidence illustrates that some of these male workers also seemed determined to only accept their women counterparts on an inferior basis. Some openly contended that these women were contributing to male unemployment and mentioned that women were not suitable for the job. Based on the evidence uncovered in this analysis, it is not surprising that it took the rise of women in leadership positions within AC Transit and ATU 192 to fundamentally change how work/life issues were addressed within this workplace.

It is also likely that responses to affirmative action pressures to hire women were greatly influenced by racial bias as well as the assumption that employers and unions were receiving the laziest and most unproductive segment of the racial minority population. Many transit companies including AC Transit actively recruited workers from the welfare programs and clearly assumed that these new workers who were predominately African American women were unfit to labor. Therefore, the unresponsiveness to the concerns voiced by the newly hired African American women workers not only reflected race and gender bias, but also class bias.

In turn, newly hired African American women transit operators who thought that they gained access to opportunity soon realize that they entered a hostile territory where their structure of opportunity was heavily influenced by omnipresent surveillance as well as disparate discipline and punishment. Their hard work was not enough to change their stress-laden and increasingly precarious work conditions. Showing up to work early did not make the work pressure and truncated autonomy they endured lessen. Making matters worse, instead of encouraging workers to be more productive, their demanding work conditions oftentimes motivated them to employ strategies to cope with work abuses and work/life imbalances that had devastating consequences.

African American women workers secured transit operator positions while the occupation was still considered a coveted job, especially for the chosen and gap-fillers like White women and African American men who gained access to the job during and after the World War II era. While African American women benefited from ATU 192's advocacy at times, their employment rewards and job security were mitigated by lingering concerns about their personhood, industry-wide changes in the labor process, macrostructural shifts influenced by neoliberalism that have undermined the impact of union membership, as well as the treatment of workers in this country. As tightrope walkers, African American women and similarly situated transit operators did not have at their disposal the tools necessary to protect themselves from abuse both within the workplace as well as within the union. Those among the chosen were able to protect themselves from worker abuse by creating a seniority system within the union that institutionalized their privilege over other workers within the firm. Many of the gap-fillers who stuck with the job were also able to utilize the seniority system and use it to their advantage. Nevertheless, by the time African American women gained access to the job in large numbers, seniority was in the process of becoming less meaningful due to external economic pressures on the firm as well as internal conflicts among union members and leadership.

African American women's capacity to amend factors shaping their working conditions was not only undermined by persistent race-, sex-, and class-based antagonisms but also by institutional actions. AC Transit profoundly dismantled the impact of Affirmative Action legislation and goals by restructuring the work process through its (1) creation and/ or maintenance of a two-tiered system of employment relations, (2) implementation of neoliberal employment arrangements, and by (3) utilization of bureaucratic policies that were disproportionately applied within the workplace.

Impact of Two-Tiered Employment Relations

AC Transit began restructuring the work process through its creation of a two-tiered system of employment relations the workplace. AC Transit created Dial-A-Ride positions in Richmond, California, in 1974 and began disproportionately placing African American women in these positions. By 1975, Black women operators made up 80 percent of the full-time transit operators placed upon hire at the Richmond Division. Evidence from the ATU 192 records indicate that AC Transit made very little effort to make the Dial-a-Ride operations bearable for those transit operators hired to provide services in Richmond and other poor communities in the East Bay area. AC Transit altered the transit operating held by workers assigned to the Dial-a-Ride program by removing breaks during the workday. Dial-a-Ride operators were not allowed to take breaks while picking up patrons for this service in addition to when they were driving other lines operated by the district. AC Transit maintained that the labor contract did not specifically state that Dial-a-Ride operators had a right to breaks. It took Labor Arbitrator William Eaton to rule that Dial-a-Ride operators had a right to break time during the workday, given that AC Transit had a long history of providing "spot" or break time to workers placed at other divisions within the firm.

Impact of Neoliberal Employment Arrangements

African American women transit operators also made up a significant portion of the new part-time workers hired by AC Transit, especially during the early 1980s. Part-time transit operators have a long history of struggle as AC Transit workers. ATU 192 records indicate that by 1989, some of them had been working split shifts for three years and did not have health insurance. Part-time operators were typically hired to work four to six hours a day during morning or evening shifts. While they earned good wages with AC Transit, they did not have access to vacation time, sick leave, or health insurance.

AC Transit's attempt to limit opportunities available to new hires after 1974 did not end with its placement and recovery policies. This firm also began to reconstitute race and gender inequality in this job by including a new pay progression schedule in 1975, which stipulated that new workers would not receive top pay until one year after hire. Over the years, the pay progression has increased substantially. As Ruth puts it, "times have changed since I came through. When I came through, I started October 14. I completed my training November 22. [After that time,] I was considered a 'full on probation employee.' I was on probation for 90 days and after 90 days I was considered a full time, top pay employee, just like everyone else that was working. Now, things have changed. You have to go 3 and a half years before you can get the top pay."

In addition to forcing transit operators to work out of classification and failing to compensate them for working beyond their pay grade, AC Transit instituted new run schedules that jeopardized the transit worker's ability to keep the job, especially women workers who are single parents. Transit operators enjoyed straight through runs until 1974. But after this time, AC Transit redesigned its run structure by creating a schedule that mimicked industrial standards at the time, wherein 60 percent of the runs during the weekdays were split shifts. By the mid-1980s, AC Transit expanded its use of split shifts by increasing its use of these shifts to 80 percent of the runs during weekdays. As a result, before and after receiving dependent care assistance from AC Transit, many working mothers and caregivers of elderly parents continue to struggle in their attempts to balance the unpredictability of work and family responsibilities.

Role of Bureaucratic Policies and Discipline Disparities

AC Transit's efforts to restructure the labor process shortened workers' longevity on the job and increased their vulnerability to stress, loss of employment, and occupational injury. Many stressors were also spurred by human resource policies designed to curb attendance problems. On the surface, efforts to curb absentee rates are not unique, particularly when they are evenly applied to address excessive absences throughout the workplace. However, evidence demonstrates that AC Transit failed to implement attendance policies fairly. For instance, the attendance policy that emerged in 1983 was used to sanction and discharge workers who were not even aware of the policy's existence. ATU 192 had to take this issue to arbitration before AC Transit made efforts to correct its application and disproportionate implementation of this policy across divisions. AC Transit in this arbitration was also forced to rescind the harsh discipline it imposed on injured workers who were fired, despite having suffered the injury on the job. Workers who hoped to avoid discipline would show up sick and/or injured to work. On the contrary, other sick or injured workers began to watch their sanctions mount for excessive absences.

The Grand Jury Report alongside the correspondence and arbitrations from the ATU 192 records illustrate how AC Transit contributed to the increasing rate of illness and injury among transit operators by purchasing defective equipment, as well as refusing to hire, train, and retain maintenance workers. AC Transit had even gone as far as imposing harsh penalties on workers who were operating faulty equipment that contributed to public disasters. It is also clear from union arbitrations as well as the discipline reports that the divisions with a heavy concentration of women and African American workers were disciplined much more harshly than those dominated by White male transit operators. While Newark transit operators were given adverse warnings for "failures to report," operators at the East Oakland and Richmond districts received light to heavy suspensions for failing to show up to work.

Although AC Transit succeeded in hiring previously excluded workers, this transit employer began to govern over these workers with the assumption that the fear of discipline would provoke compliance among those who cared to keep the job and expose those workers who were unfit. Until compelled to respond to industrial injuries and stress, this transit company made minimal effort to make the job safe for the workers they employed. Instead, AC Transit watched industrial injuries mount that could have been prevented and dismissed the workers who could not overcome these hurdles. While this study was not designed to uncover whether AC Transit intentionally tried to set workers up to fail, the findings certainly support the claim that when industrial injuries and stress mounted for workers, AC Transit actively worked to deflect responsibility and attribute productivity problems to worker morale and misconduct. Transit operators like Monica who have worked for AC Transit for almost two decades contend that this organizational rush to deflect responsibility and discipline workers emerged after AC Transit began hiring more women and racial minority workers.

Former ATU 192 President Ely Hill agrees with Monica's contention. Hill noted in a 1990 interview that transit operating jobs once were easy jobs that were relaxed, particularly compared to the jobs that most African American workers held. However, after racial minorities began working these jobs in large numbers, Hill recalled that "all of a sudden they were moved to say 'You all don't come to work. What's the problem?' It's not us that's having the problem, it's you having the problem as soon as I got here. When it was all really White, everything was fine and dandy. . . . But now that I'm inside, here comes the bottom falling out."[2] Hill contended in his interview that if AC Transit was serious about improving the morale and stress levels of workers, it needed to start treating workers like human beings, making efforts to stop placing all of the budgetary strain on the drivers, and it would need to begin recognizing the challenges of sick workers and single mothers. Hill also mentioned that AC Transit should cease its attempts to be "the doctor and the judge, when it only wants to issue out the discipline."[3]

Where Do We Go From Here?

Employment insecurity is not only a problem that transit workers face. In recent years, employment insecurity is like a plague that affects many workers, especially those who have less marketable skills as well as those workers who went to college and secured a graduate education only to land jobs as involuntary part-time service workers. Millions of American workers feel betrayed because employers have turned the socioeconomic and psychological rewards of meritocracy into empty promises that include declining real wages, expensive fringe benefits, and unaddressed work/life conflicts. In this era of neoliberalism, workers have become increasingly vulnerable to workplace abuse and must work harder than in previous years to make ends meet.

It is not a secret that paths to economic stability and job security have been truncated by economic greed. However, data in this study suggest that employment security has been further compromised by organizational responses to external pressures to desegregate workforces and develop nondiscriminatory ways of engaging previously excluded workers. The "plantation style of management" that emerged in response to demographic shifts has gone unchecked. Countless workers contend with constant monitoring and are increasingly subjected to rules that lead to dismissal. Nevertheless, we still have not figured out how to bring employers and unions back into the conversations about how best to ward off poverty and employment insecurity. Instead, national conversations about the workplace have been redirected to discussions regarding the need for union representation, even in financially strapped states like Michigan and Indiana. Apparently, lawmakers in states including Michigan, Indiana, and most recently Missouri are of the assumption that enacting right-to-work laws that ensure that no person can be compelled to join a union or pay dues to a labor union can create budget surpluses and stable local economies. How is this focus our best option? Have unions outlived their purpose?

By helping workers secure the forty-hour workweek, benefits, and safe conditions, unions have been instrumental in transforming the American workplace for the better. However, with the emergence of federal and state labor departments and agencies like the Occupational Safety and Health Administration, some have argued that unions have outlived their purpose. While unions complain about "free riders" and other concerns that undermine their capacity to represent workers, proponents of right-to-work legislation contend that unions have lost their way and purpose within American society.

The problem with these assumptions about unions goes beyond the claim that these organizations are self-interested and solely concerned with growing their political clout. The most problematic component of the attacks against unions is the assumption that they exist to protect lazy workers from termination. Notwithstanding the increasing wealth gap between working Americans and top company bosses who receive bonuses even when their companies are failing, political pundits have been busy blaming the country's problems on workers and families that are assumed to be more dependent on government programs than a decent day's work. While unions have been casted as parasites that are sucking the blood from defenseless employers, the real aim of the attack against unions has been focused on undermining the need to advocate for workers, who are characterized as incompetent and lazy.

Although proponents of the right-to-work legislation claim to care about workers forced to join unions and pay union dues, they have focused less attention on the increasingly stressful and harmful workplace conditions that generate the need for union representation. Decades of research illustrate that American workers are experiencing escalating stress and increasing job demands.[4] Neoliberal employment practices which are credited with improving the nation's economic health including outsourcing, rapid business expansion, and downsizing have created a host of stress-related problems for workers. Gone are the days when white-collar workers could do their job and leave it at the workplace and when semiskilled workers could expect autonomy and job stability. The days of set schedules and predictability on the job have been replaced with odd hours and rotating shifts set to meet the demands of commerce and destined to undermine the health and career prospects of workers. High-stress jobs also affect employees' life circumstances because the remnants of experiences and pressures shouldered while busy at work lingers from the job to the home. Researchers have linked persistent stress to suppressed immune system function, diabetes, impaired memory, sleep deprivation, as well as psychological challenges including depression and anxiety conditions. Workers in high-stress situations are also more likely to experience family dysfunction and divorce.[5]

In addition to the aforementioned pressures, workers in high-stress occupations like transit operating jobs can tell horror stories that play out at work about how motorists bob and weave through traffic and stop suddenly, as well as those who foolishly stop traffic to seek directions. Combined with the pressure of traffic and work rules that encourage employees to sacrifice rest periods for the good of the service, AC Transit workers can add to the horror the numbing realities of being forced to work with equipment that causes physical pain. They have also contended with surprise attacks from teenagers, angry passengers, and unruly people traveling to and from their drug and mental health appointments. Without the assistance of unions, workers in high-stress positions run the risk of facing workplace stressors in an uncertain economy alone.

Recent publicized cases of corporate abuse of power have reignited a debate over public control over big corporations. But, the media debate over the missions of corporations and the actions of double-dealing chief executive officers has not unearthed any new revelations about corporation mismanagement; in fact, many commentators on the recent corporate scandals have taken the stance that corporate greed is a minuscule problem that has only ruined a handful of firms in the business community. Political commentators have conveniently subsumed the problem to one wherein there are just a few "bad apples" that deserve swift punishment because they are ruining the public's confidence in the business community.

This extended case study illustrates that our worries about the business world need to be extended beyond the actions of big corporations and should be concerned with the deeds of businesses whose operations are as vulnerable to local level stereotypes and biases as they are to macrostructural elements like globalization. Despite federal and state pressure to integrate the workforce, employers like AC Transit did not make the necessary adjustments to help ensure the rights of minority workers. Instead, as illustrated in this study, AC Transit managers made shifts in the organization of work within this workplace that reinforced the existing hierarchies and changed the culture of opportunity within this firm. In turn, many of the African American women workers in this study report that their opportunities have been cut short because they were never extended the "benefit of a doubt."

Evidence from this study also illustrates the extent to which the changes in the organization of work, in addition to the increasing implementation of arbitrary moral standards in human resource management policies, have served to individualize the structural limitations to upward mobility and also have served to justify America's failed commitment to equal opportunity since the Civil Rights era. Scholars interested in public sector jobs stand to uncover much more about how controlling images became institutionalized by focusing on variations of collective bargaining rights enforcement within and between occupations. Scholars would also benefit from analyzing the extent to which the practice of defunding public services is related to shifts in the demographic makeup of these workforces and the populations they serve.[6] Additionally, further study in this area will benefit from attempts to make distinctions between the circumstances shaping inequality within low-skilled jobs in which women and racial minority workers are overcrowded as well as unequal trends in high-skilled jobs in which women and racial minority workers are underrepresented.[7]

That said, the news is not all bad. Some good developments are emerging out of the flattening structure of opportunity described in this study. Within declining industries like urban mass transit that depend on public funding, labor organizations and transit consumers have joined forces. Although influential civil rights victories helped working-class people gain the right to sit where they desire on the bus, the conditions of urban bus transit in many communities from New York to Chicago and the San Francisco Bay Area are less than desirable for the bus patrons as well as the transit operators who are predominately people of color. Urban bus systems have spiraled downward since the 1970s due to inadequate bus service that limits bus patron's access to better paying jobs and undermines their ability to get to the jobs they do have on time. While urban transit districts are responsible for providing quality services to patrons and an equitable and safe working environment, the people of Alameda County and other underserved communities throughout the nation have in part regional transportation agencies like the Metropolitan Transportation Commission to thank for the decline in services. Since the Metropolitan Transportation Commission controls the purse strings and determines how state and federal transit dollars are allocated, its decision to persist in privileging rail transit over bus transit has had a devastating influence on the funds available to bus transit as well as the quality of services available to the people who depend on this public service. In the East Bay area, BART and Caltrain are commuter services that primarily serve White and affluent patrons who need transportation from the suburbs to major downtown business districts. Seventy-five percent of BART patrons make over $30,000 and 53 percent of Caltrain passengers earn more than $75,000 a year. They also have cars and are not as transit-dependent as bus transit patrons. Eighty percent of BART riders and 83 percent of Caltrain commuters owned automobiles in 2005,[8] while almost 60 percent of AC Transit bus riders were completely transit-dependent with "no means of transportation other than public transit to get to essential destinations, such as jobs, school, grocery stores, and social services."[9] Eighty percent of bus patrons were people of color and 30 percent of AC Transit bus patrons earn less than $25,000 a year.[10]

Despite the original intent of UMTA to serve the citizens who rely on mass transit, the federal funding priorities have privileged commuters who are not transit-dependent. AC Transit passengers get a subsidy of federal funding of $2.78 per trip in 2005, while BART riders received $6.14 and Caltrain received $13.79 per trip.[11] The funding disparities privileging rail transit commuters have led to an expansion of services available to rail commuter patrons. For bus transit, funding disparities have contributed to a 30 percent reduction in services over the last thirty years in addition to increased fares and a dependence on dilapidated bus fleets that make transit-reliant patrons chronically late for work, school, as well as social service and medical appointments.[12]

Due to the disparities that manifested within the urban transit industry since the 1970s, organizations from transit unions to environmental groups have joined forces to fight to improve the quality of public transportation because this effort will help the workers as well as the transit-reliant communities. Bus transit unions emerged in places like Los Angeles to defend bus patron's right to a safe, secure, and reliable public transportation system. Representing a community wherein about 65 percent had incomes under $15,000, the Bus Riders Union in Los Angeles formed in 1989. In addition to advocating for bettering working conditions for transit operators, Bus Riders Unions in Los Angeles as well as others throughout the nation including Atlanta's T-Riders Union and the New York–based West Harlem for Environmental Action have been busy working to secure replacements for old diesel buses with compressed natural gas buses and opposing attempts to raise fares and eliminate unlimited use bus passes. As such, the struggle to advocate for the rights of working-class people and the communities they serve lives on.[13]

Notes

Abbreviations

ATU 192 Collection	Labor Archives Research Center (LARC) Amalgamated Transit Union, Local 192 Records, Larc.Ms.0327, Labor Archives and Research Center, San Francisco State University
Bancroft Collection	Bancroft Library: University of California, Berkeley
FTA FOIA Records	Freedom of Information Act (FOIA) Request to U.S. Department of Transportation, Federal Transit Administration, file no. 10-0149
NARA, SF	National Archives and Records Administration, San Francisco
Sam Kagel Collection, LARC	Sam Kagel Collection, folder 7806, Labor Archives and Research Center, San Francisco State University

Introduction

1. Sylvia Ann Hewlett, *Off-Ramps and On-Ramps: Keeping Talented Women on the Road to Success* (Cambridge, MA: Harvard Business School, 2007); Arlie Russell Hochschild, *The Time Bind: When Work Becomes Home and Home Becomes Work*, 2nd ed. (New York: Henry Holt, 2001); Arlie Russell Hochschild, *The Outsourced Self: Intimate Life in Market Times* (New York: Metropolitan Books, 2013).

2. African American women's progress in semiskilled professions has received limited attention. However, a few well-researched exceptions exist. See Enobough Hannah Branch, *Opportunity Denied: Limiting Black Women to Devalued Work* (New Brunswick, NJ: Rutgers University Press, 2011); Marion Swerdlow, "Men's Accommodations to Women Entering a Nontraditional Occupation: A Case of Rapid Transit Operatives," *Gender & Society* 3 (1989): 373–381; Jacqueline Jones, *Labor of Love, Labor of Sorrow: Black Women, Work, and the Family, from Slavery to the Present* (New York: Basic Books, 1985).

3. Augustin Kwasi Fosu, "Occupational Gains of Black Women Since the 1964 Civil Rights Act: Long-Term or Episodic?" *American Economic Review* 87, no. 2 (1997): 311–314; Tera W. Hunter, *To "Joy My Freedom": Southern Black Women's Lives and Labors after the Civil War* (Cambridge, MA: Harvard University Press, 1997); Phyllis Ann Wallace, *Black Women in the Labor Force* (Cambridge, MA: MIT Press, 1980); Randy P. Albelda, "Occupational Segregation by Race and Gender, 1958–1981," *Industrial and Labor Relations Review* 39, no. 3 (1986): 404–411.

4. Mary C. King, "Human Capital and Black Women's Occupational Mobility," *Industrial Relations* 34, no. 2 (1995): 282–298.

5. Eileen Appelbaum, Annette Bernhardt, and Richard J. Murnane, eds., *Low-Wage America: How Employers Are Reshaping Opportunity in the Workplace* (New York: Russell Sage, 2003); Randy Albelda, "Fallacies of Welfare-to-Work Policies," *Annals of the American Academy of Political and Social Science* 577 (2001): 66–78; Natalie J. Sokoloff, *Black Women and White Women in the Professions: Occupational Segregation by Race and Gender, 1960–1980* (New York: Routledge, 1992); Bette Woody, *Black Women in the New Services Economy: Help or Hindrance in Economic Self-Sufficiency?* (Wellesley, MA: Wellesley College, Center for Research on Women, 1989).

6. Richard Lempert, "A Personal Odyssey toward a Theme: Race and Equality in the United States: 1948–2009," *Law and Society Review* 44 (2010): 431–462; Laura Dresser, "To Be Young, Black, and Female: Falling Further Behind in a Shifting Economy," *Dollars and Sense* (May/June 1995): 32–34; Sokoloff, *Black Women and White Women in the Professions.*

7. Catherine M. Casserly, *African American Women and Poverty: Can Education Alone Change the Status Quo?* (New York: Garland Pub, 1998), 3.

8. Christine Bose, Roslyn Feldberg, and Natalie Sokoloff, *Hidden Aspects of Women's Work*, ed. Bose, Feldberg, and Sokoloff with the Women and Work Research Group (New York: Praeger, 1987), 23.

9. Raine Dozier, "The Declining Relative Status of Black Women Workers, 1980–2002," *Social Forces* 88, no. 4 (2010): 1833–1857; David M. Autor, Lawrence F. Katz, and Melissa S. Kearney, "Trends in U.S. Wage Inequality: A Re-Assessment of the Revisionists," NBER Working Paper 11627 (Cambridge, MA: National Bureau of Economic Research, 2004); Irene Browne and Joya Misra, "The Intersection of Gender and Race in the Labor Market," *Annual Review of Sociology* 29 (2003): 487–513. Jones, *Labor of Love, Labor of Sorrow.*

10. Michael Kompier and Vittorio Di Martino, "Review of Bus Drivers' Occupational Stress and Stress Prevention," *Stress Medicine* 11 (1995): 253–262; D. R. Ragland, B. A. Greiner, and J. M. Fisher, "Studies of Health Outcomes in Transit Operators: Policy Implications of Current Scientific Database," *Journal of Occupational Health Psychology* 3 (1998): 172–187; Marilyn Winkleby, "Occupational Stressors and Hypertension Microform: A Study of San Francisco Bus Drivers" (PhD diss., University of California, Berkeley, 1986).

11. Arne L. Kalleberg, "Nonstandard Employment Relations: Part-Time, Temporary, and Contract Work," *Annual Review of Sociology* 26 (2000): 341–365; Chris Tilly, *Half a Job: Bad and Good Part-Time Jobs in a Changing Labor Market* (Philadelphia: Temple University Press, 1996); Jon Gabel, "Job-Based Health Insurance, 1977–1998: The Accidental System under Scrutiny," *Health Affairs* 18, no. 6 (1999): 62–74; Frances Fox Piven and Richard A. Cloward, *Regulating the Poor: The Functions of Public Welfare* (New York: Vintage Books, 1993).

12. Michael Katz, *Undeserving Poor: From the War on Poverty to the War on Welfare* (New York: Knopf Doubleday Publishing Group, 1989).

13. Stephan Thernstrom and Abigail Thernstrom, *America in Black and White: One Nation, Indivisible* (New York: Simon & Schuster, 1997); Nathan Glazer and

Daniel Patrick Moynihan, *Beyond the Melting Pot: The Negroes, Puerto Ricans, Jews, Italians, and Irish of New York City*, 2nd ed. (Cambridge, MA: MIT Press, 1970); Nan L. Maxwell, "Occupational Differences in the Determination of U.S. Workers' Earnings: Both the Human Capital and the Structured Labor Market Hypotheses Are Useful in Analysis," *American Journal of Economics and Sociology* 46, no. 4 (1987): 431–443.

Chapter 1

1. Sheldon Danziger and Peter Gottschalk, *America Unequal* (Cambridge, MA: Harvard University Press, 1995); William Julius Wilson, *When Work Disappears: The World of the New Ghetto Poor* (New York: Knoff, 1996); Barry Bluestone, Mary Stevenson, and Chris Tilly, "An Assessment of the Impact of 'Deindustrialization' and Spatial Mismatch on the Labor Market Outcomes of Young White, Black, and Latino Men and Women Who Have Limited Schooling" (working paper, John W. McCormack Institute of Public Affairs, University of Massachusetts-Boston, 1992). Barry Bluestone and Bennett Harrison, *The Deindustrialization of America: Plant Closings, Community Abandonment, and the Dismantling of Basic Industry* (New York: Basic Books, 1982).

2. U.S. Bureau of Economic Analysis, *National Income and Product Accounts of the United States* (Washington, DC: U.S. Department of Commerce, 2004), tables 6.8 B and C.

3. Vernon Mogensen, ed., *Worker Safety under Siege: Labor, Capital, and the Politics of Workplace Safety in a Deregulated World* (Armonk, NY: M. E. Sharpe, 2006); Paul D. Carrington and Trina Jones, *Law and Class in America: Trends since the Cold War* (New York: New York University Press, 2006); Frances Fox Piven and Richard A. Cloward, *Regulating the Poor: The Functions of Public Welfare* (New York: Vintage Books, 1993).

4. Clair Brown, John Haltiwanger, and Julia Lane, *Economic Turbulence: Is a Volatile Economy Good for America?* (Chicago: The University of Chicago Press, 2006), 37.

5. Eileen Appelbaum, Annette Bernhardt, and Richard J. Murnane, eds., *Low-Wage America: How Employers Are Reshaping Opportunity in the Workplace* (New York: Russell Sage, 2003).

6. U.S. Bureau of Labor Statistics, *National Employment, Hours, and Earnings: Average Weekly Hours of Production Workers: SIC 701—Hotels and Motels* (Washington, DC: U.S. Department of Labor, 2002).

7. Appelbaum et al., *Low-Wage America*; Nancy Foner, *The Caregiving Dilemma: Work in an American Nursing Home* (Berkeley: University of California Press, 1994).

8. Neil Fligstein, *The Architecture of Markets: An Economic Sociology of Twenty-First-Century Capitalist Societies* (Princeton, NJ: Princeton University Press, 2001).

9. Ryan A. Smith and James R. Elliott, "Does Ethnic Concentration Influence Employees' Access to Authority? An Examination of Contemporary Urban Labor Markets," *Social Forces* 81 (2002): 255–279; Eric Grodsky and Devah Pager, "The Structure of Disadvantage: Individual and Occupational Determinants of the

Black-White Wage Gap," *American Sociological Review* 66 (2001): 542–567; Donald Tomaskovic-Devey, "The Gender and Race Composition of Jobs and Male/Female, White/Black Pay Gaps," *Social Forces* 72 (1993): 45–76; Barbara Reskin and Patricia Roos, *Job Queues, Gender Queues: Explaining Women's Inroads into Male Occupations* (Philadelphia: Temple University, 1990); Phyllis Ann Wallace, *Black Women in the Labor Force* (Cambridge, MA: MIT Press, 1980).

10. Hurbert M. Blalock, *Towards a Theory of Minority Group Relations* (New York: Wiley, 1967).

11. Vincent J. Roscigno, Lisette M. Garcia, and Donna Bobbitt-Zeher, "Social Closure and Processes of Race/Sex Employment Discrimination," *Annals of the American Academy of Political and Social Science* 609 (2007): 16–48; Laura Perna, "Sex and Race Differences in Faculty Tenure and Promotion," *Research in Higher Education* 42, no. 5 (2001): 541–567; Grodsky and Pager, "The Structure of Disadvantage"; Marlese Durr and John R. Logan, "Racial Submarkets in Government Employment: African American Managers in New York State," *Sociological Forum* 12, no. 3 (1997): 353–370.

12. Marianne Bertrand and Sendhil Mullainathan, "Are Emily and Greg More Employable than Lakisha and Jamal? A Field Experiment on Labor Market Discrimination," *American Economic Review* 94, no. 4 (2004): 991–1013; Phillip Moss and Chris Tilly, *Stories Employers Tell: Race, Skill, and Hiring in America* (New York: Russell Sage, 2001); Kathryn M. Neckerman and Joleen Kirschenman, "Hiring Strategies, Racial Bias, and Inner-City Workers," *Social Problems* 38, no. 4 (1991): 433–447.

13. Ivy Kennelly, "'That Single-Mother Element': How White Employers Typify Black Women," *Gender and Society* 13, no. 2 (1999): 168–192.

14. Erin L. Kelly, Phyllis Moen, J. Michael Oakes, Wen Fan, Cassandra Okechukwu, Kelly D. Davis, Leslie B. Hammer, et al., "Changing Work and Work-Family Conflict: Evidence from the Work, Family, and Health Network," *American Sociological Review* 79, no. 3 (June 2014): 485–516; Mary C. Noonan and Mary E. Corcoran, "The Mommy Track and Partnership: Temporary Delay or Dead End?" *Annals of the American Academy of Political and Social Science* 596 (Nov. 2004): 130–150; Rosemary Batt and Monique P. Valcour, "Human Resources Practices as Predictors of Work-Family Outcomes and Employee Turnover," *Industrial Relations* 42 (2003): 189–220; Jerry A. Jacobs and Kathleen Gerson, *The Time Divide: Work, Family, and Gender Inequality* (Cambridge, MA: Harvard University Press, 2004); Noelle Chesley, "Blurring Boundaries? Linking Technology Use, Spillover, Individual Distress, and Family Satisfaction," *Journal of Marriage and Family* 67 (2005): 1237–1248; Daphne Spain and Susan M. Bianchi, *Balancing Act: Motherhood, Marriage, and Employment among American Women* (New York: Russell Sage Foundation, 1996).

15. James N. Baron and Andrew E. Newman, "Pay the Man: Effects of Demographic Composition on Prescribed Pay Rates in the California Civil Service," in *Pay Equity: Empirical Inquiries*, ed. Robert T. Michael, Heidi Hartmann, and Bridget O'Farrell (Washington, DC: National Academy Press, 1989), 107–130; Joan R.

Acker, "Hierarchies, Jobs, Bodies: A Theory of Gendered Organizations," *Gender & Society* 4 (1990): 139–158.

16. Bluestone and Harrison, *The Deindustrialization of America*; David Cornfield, "Declining Union Membership in the Post–World War II Era: The United Furniture Workers of America, 1939–1982," *American Journal of Sociology* 91 (1986): 1112–1153; Sanford M. Jacoby, "Norms and Cycles: The Dynamics of Non-Union Industrial Relations in the United States, 1897–1987," in *New Developments in the Labor Market*, ed. K. Abraham and R. McKersie (Cambridge, MA: MIT Press, 1990), 19–57.

17. John Bound and Laura Dresser, "Losing Ground: The Erosion of the Relative Earnings of African American Women during the 1980s," in *Latinas and African American Women at Work*, ed. Irene Browne (New York: Russell Sage Foundation, 1999), 73–74.

18. Donald Tomaskovic-Devey and Kevin Stainback, "Discrimination and Desegregation: Equal Opportunity Progress in U.S. Private Sector Workplaces since the Civil Rights Act," *Annals of the American Academy of Political and Social Science* 609 (2007): 49–84; Roscigno et al., "Social Closure and Processes of Race/ Sex Employment Discrimination."

19. Paula England, Joan M. Hermsen, and David A. Cotter, "The Devaluation of Women's Work: A Comment on Tam," *American Journal of Sociology* 105 (2000): 1741–1760; Trond Petersen and Laurie A. Morgan, "Separate and Unequal: Occupation-Establishment Sex Segregation and the Gender Wage Gap," *American Journal of Sociology* 101 (1995): 329–365; Barbara Kilbourne, Paula England, and Kurt Beron, "Effects of Individual, Occupational, and Industrial characteristics on Earnings: Intersections of Race and Gender," *Social Forces* 72, no. 4 (1994): 1149–1176; Cynthia H. Chertos, Lois Haigrere, and Ronnie Steinberg, *Occupational Segregation and Its Impact on Working Women: A Conference Report of a Conference Held at the Ford Foundation, June 9, 1982* (Albany, NY: Center for Women in Government, State University at Albany, 1982); Shelley Coverman, "Occupational Sectoration and Sex Differences in Earnings," *Research in Social Stratification and Mobility* 5 (1986): 139–172.

20. William B. Gould, *Black Workers in White Unions: Job Discrimination in the United States* (Ithaca, NY: Cornell University Press, 1977).

21. Bill Fletcher Jr., "The Imperative of Black Worker Mobilization in Renewing Organized Labor in the United States," in *Race and Labor Matters in the New U.S. Economy*, ed. Manning Marable Immanuel Ness and Joseph Wilson (Lanham, MD: Rowman & Littlefield Publishers, 2006), 22.

22. Dorothy Sue Cobble, "Rethinking Troubled Relations between Women and Unions: Craft Unionism and Female Activism," *Feminist Studies* 16, no. 3 (Autumn 1990): 519–548; Ruth Milkman, "Organizing the Sexual Division of Labor: Historical Perspectives on Women's Work and the American Labor Movement," *Socialist Review* 49 (Jan.-Feb. 1980): 95–150.

23. Marion Crane, "Women, Labor Unions, and Hostile Work Environments: The Untold Story," *Texas Journal of Women and Law* 9 (1995): 66–77.

24. Annette Bernhardt, Ruth Milkman, Nik Theodore, Douglas Heckathorn, Mirabai Auer, James DeFilippis, Ana Luz Gonzalez, et al., "Broken Laws, Unprotected Workers: Violations of Employment and Labor Laws in American Cities," 2010, http://www.unprotectedworkers.org /index.php/broken_laws/index, accessed December 19, 2015; Appelbaum et al., *Low-Wage America*.

25. Evelyn Nakano Glenn, *Unequal Freedom: How Race and Gender Shaped American Citizenship and Labor* (Cambridge, MA: Harvard University Press, 2002); Patricia Hill Collins, "The Meanings of Motherhood in Black Culture and Black Mother-Daughter Relationships," in *Gender through the Prism of Difference*, ed. Maxine B. Zinn, Pierrette Hondagneu-Sotelo, and Michael Messner (New York: Oxford University Press, 2010), 285–295; Patricia Hill Collins, *Black Feminist Thought: Knowledge, Consciousness, and the Politics of Empowerment* (Boston: Unwin Hyman, 1990).

26. Naomi Gerstel and Dan Clawson, "Class Advantage and the Gender Divide: Flexibility on the Job and at Home," *American Journal of Sociology* 120, no. 2 (Sept. 2014): 409.

27. Charles Ragin and David Zaret, "Theory and Method in Comparative Research: Two Strategies," *Social Forces* 61, no. 3 (1983): 731–754.

28. Joleen Kirschenman and Kathryn M. Neckerman, "We'd Love to Hire Them, but . . .": The Meaning of Race for Employers," in *The Urban Underclass*, ed. Christopher Jencks and Paul E. Peterson (Washington, DC: Brookings Institution, 1991), 203–232; Harry J. Holzer, *What Employers Want: Job Prospects for Less-Educated Workers* (New York: Russell Sage Foundation, 1997).

29. Robin Stryker, "Disparate Impact and the Quota Debates: Law, Labor Market Sociology, and Equal Employment Policies," *Sociological Quarterly* 42 (2001): 13–46. David B. Wilkins and G. Mitu Gulati, "Why Are There So Few Black Lawyers in Corporate Law Firms? An Institutional Analysis," *California Law Review* 84, no. 3 (1996): 493–625; Barbara J. Flagg, "Fashioning a Title VII Remedy for Transparently White Subjective Decision Making," *Yale Law Journal* 104, no. 8 (1995): 2009–2051.

30. David Harvey, "Crafting the Neoliberal State: Workfare, Prisonfare, and Social Insecurity," *Sociological Forum* 25, no. 2 (2007): 197–220; Pierre Bourdieu, *The Social Structures of the Economy* (Cambridge: Polity Press, 2005).

31. Pierre Bourdieu, *Practical Reason: On the Theory of Action* (Palo Alto: Stanford University Press, 1998).

32. Much of this trend is due to the work of corporate-funded think tanks that convinced the American electorate and their representatives to individualize the causes of poverty, rather than address the structural causes of workplace inequality. Business-funded think tanks like the American Enterprise Institute, which was established in 1970, the Heritage Foundation that opened in 1973, and the Manhattan Institute that opened in 1977 issued reports that challenged the consequences of increasing poverty relief. Most of the research generated by scholars in the think tanks advocated against expanding social welfare programs because the supporters of this research were convinced that welfare and government regulation generated a culture of dependency. By individualizing poverty and pro-

moting personal responsibility, these researchers contended that the best medicine for the poor was mandatory work programs geared to help recipients transition from welfare to work. See Manning Marable, *Race, Reform, and Rebellion: The Second Reconstruction in Black America, 1945–1990* (Jackson: University Press of Mississippi, 1991), 181; Piven and Cloward, *Regulating the Poor*, 369–370.

33. Although domestics were encouraged to limit questions and unsolicited dialogue, the domestic workers Rollins interviewed mentioned that employers had a tendency to ask "very personal questions" about their marital situations and their finances that made them uncomfortable. As one of Rollins's respondents put it, "they want to know all of your business so they know just where you're coming from. They tell you some of their problems so that you'll tell them your business. [But] it's knowledge for control they want. They're uneasy if they don't know enough about you, if they don't know what you're thinking." Judith Rollins, *Between Women: Domestics and Their Employers* (Philadelphia: Temple University Press, 1985), 164.

34. John Gilliom, *Surveillance, Privacy, and the Law: Employee Drug Testing and the Politics of Social Control* (Ann Arbor: University of Michigan, 1994), 1.

35. National Institute for Occupational Safety and Health, "Worker Health Chartbook. Chapter 2: Fatal and Nonfatal Injuries and Selected Illnesses and Conditions," 2004, http://www.cdc.gov/niosh/docs/2004-146/pdfs/2004-146.pdf, accessed December 18, 2015; Karen Messing, Katherine Lippel, Diane Demers, and Donna Mergler, "Equality and Difference in the Workplace: Physical Job Demands, Occupational Illnesses, and Sex Differences," *National Women's Studies Association Journal* 12, no. 3 (Autumn 2000): 21–49.

36. Herbert Hill, *Black Labor and the American Legal System: Race, Work, and the Law* (Madison: University of Wisconsin Press, 1977); Philip W. Jeffress, *The Negro in the Urban Transit Industry* (Philadelphia: University of Pennsylvania Press, 1970).

37. Gould, *Black Workers in White Unions*, 19.

38. Timothy Minchin, "Black Activism, the 1964 Civil Rights Act, and the Racial Integration of the Southern Textile Industry," *Journal of Southern History* 65, no. 4 (1999): 809–844.

39. Ibid., 842.

40. Jeffress, *The Negro in the Urban Transit Industry*.

41. Ibid.

42. Hill, *Black Labor and the American Legal System*, 281.

43. Fernando E. Gapasin, "Race, Gender and Other 'Problems of Unity' for the American Working Class," *Race, Gender & Class* 4, no. 1 (1996): 41–61.

44. Ibid., 46.

45. Olivia Allen-Price, "Report: You Need to Earn $29.83 an Hour to Afford a 1-Bedroom in San Francisco," KQED. March 28, 2014, http://ww2.kqed.org/news/2014/03/27/how-much-to-afford-a-1-bedroom-apartment-in-san-francisco/, accessed December 18, 2015; Bureau of Labor Statistics, U.S. Department of Labor, "Occupational Outlook Handbook, 2014–15 Edition," OOH FAQs, http://www.bls.gov/ooh/about/ooh-faqs.htm, accessed May 22, 2015.

46. Bureau of Labor Statistics, "Table 1.7 "Occupational Employment, Job Openings and Worker Characteristics" (2012).

47. Patricia A. Roos and Barbara F. Reskin, "Occupational Desegregation in the 1970s: Integration and Economic Equity?" *Sociological Perspectives* 35, no. 1 (1992): 77.

48. U.S. Census Bureau, *Statistical Abstract of the United States* (Washington, DC: U.S. Census Bureau, 2010), 396.

49. Mary Elizabeth Pidgeon. "Changes in Women's Employment During the War." *Special Bulletin No. 20 of the Women's Bureau, June* (U.S. Department of Labor, 1944), 15; U.S. Census Bureau, *Statistical Abstract of the United States*, 396.

50. The term "peculiar" used throughout this study to characterize employment relations is meant to echo the "peculiar" and contradictory nature of U.S. slavery described by sociologist Kenneth M. Stampp. See Kenneth M Stampp, *The Peculiar Institution: Slavery in the Ante-Bellum South* (New York: Knopf, 1956).

51. Alice O'Connor, Chris Tilly, and Lawrence D. Bobo, eds., *Urban Inequality: Evidence from Four Cities* (New York: Russell Sage Foundation, 2001).

52. Richard Walker, "California's Collision of Race and Class," *Representations* 55 (Summer 1996): 163–183.

53. Steven Pitts, "Black Workers in the Bay Area: Employment Trends and Job Quality: 1970 and 2000" (Berkeley: Center for Labor Research and Education, UC-Berkeley, 2006), 55.

Chapter 2

1. Complaint by Ms. Helen Capehart, Complaint 12-BR-1453 filed on January 17, 1945, RG 228, box 9, file 12-BR-1453, 228, National Archives and Records Administration (hereafter know as NARA–Pacific Region, SF).

2. Complaint by Homer L. Chambliss, Complaint 12-BR-1560 filed on November 9, 1945, RG 228, box 9, LA Transit Lines, file 12-BR-1453. 228, NARA–Pacific Region, SF.

3. Complaint by Mrs. Mary Ruth Franklin, Complaint 12-BR-1452 filed on January 12, 1945, RG 228, box 9, file 12-BR-1452, 228, p. 4, NARA–Pacific Region, SF.

4. Ibid., 2.

5. Herbert Hill, *Black Labor and the American Legal System: Race, Work, and the Law* (Madison: University of Wisconsin Press, 1977); Robert Weaver, *Negro Labor, a National Problem* (New York: Harcourt Brace, 1946), 174.

6. Weaver, *Negro Labor*, 180.

7. De Leuw, Cather & Company, Consulting Engineers, "Alameda-Contra Costa Transit District: Report on an Initial Transit Plan," December 1957, box 23, folder 12, p. 1, ATU 192 Collection, LARC.

8. Dr. Charles, "S. Johnson Survey," written on April 4, 1944, RG 228, box 2, folder statistics, p. 52, NARA–Pacific Region, SF.

9. Karen Anderson Tucker, "Last Hired, First Fired: Black Women Workers during World War II," *Journal of American History* 69, no. 1 (1982): 82–97.

10. Gretchen Lemke-Santangelo, *Abiding Courage: African American Migrant Women and the East Bay Community* (Chapel Hill: University of North Carolina Press, 1996), 108.

11. Ibid., 113.

12. Ibid., 108.

13. U.S. Bureau of Labor Statistics, *Postwar Status of Negro Workers in the San Francisco Area* (Washington, DC: U.S. Department of Labor, 1950), 614.

14. California State Employment Service, Research and Statistics Section, "Economic Status of Negroes in the San Francisco Bay Area" (May 1963), 8.

15. Dr. Charles, "S. Johnson Survey"; Robert Self, *American Babylon: Race and the Struggle for Postwar Oakland* (Princeton, NJ: Princeton University Press, 2003).

16. "Annual Report: Case Docketed from September 1, 1943 to August 31, 1944," RG 228, box 3, FEPC Virginia Seymour, NARA, SF.

17. "Letter to Franklin D. Roosevelt," written by Spencer O. Rogers, August 24 and August 26, 1943, RG 228, box 29, folder, 12-BR-59 SF Muni, Records of the War Manpower Commission (WMC), NARA–Pacific Region, SF.

18. Dr. Charles, "S. Johnson Survey," 9.

19. "Manpower Program for the Local Transit Industry," written by Joseph E. Eastmore on January 20, 1944, RG 202, 10-16986 Key System, Oakland, p. 4, NARA, SF.

20. Ibid., 4.

21. "Letter to William H. Davis," written by Joseph D. Keenan on July 17, 1944, RG 202, 10- 16986 Key System, Oakland, p. 3, NARA, SF.

22. "Complaint by Lige Webb," Complaint 12-BR-749 filed on November 13, 1945, RG 228, box 12, Key System, file 12-BR-749, NARA, SF.

23. Hill, *Black Labor and the American Legal System*, 317.

24. Ibid., 317–318.

25. Ibid., 318–319.

26. Ibid., 319.

27. "Letter to Malcolm, Ross," written on April 30, 1945, Re: Key System, Case No. 81, RG 228, box 17, 1-UR-499 Boilermakers, Local 1104 Seattle, pp: 12, 15, and 19, NARA, SF.

28. Weaver, *Negro Labor*, 188.

29. "Letter to Harry Kingman," written by Sam Kagel on July 19, 1944, RG 228, box 3, folder, Records of the War Manpower Commission (WMC) Sam Kagel/San Francisco, NARA, SF.

30. "Letter to Edward Rutledge," written to Harry L. Kingman, Re: clearance order request from the Richmond Shipyards for 5900 workers, RG 228, box 3, folder, Records of the War Manpower Commission (WMC) Sam Kagel/San Francisco, p. 2, NARA, SF.

31. Self, *American Babylon*, 48; Hill, *Black Labor and the American Legal System*, 322, 121.

32. Gretchen Lemke-Santangelo, *Abiding Courage*, 167; Edward Everett France, *Some Aspects of the Migration of the Negro to the San Francisco Bay Area since 1940* (San Francisco: R & E Research Associates, 1974), 75.

33. De Leuw, Cather & Company, "Alameda-Contra Costa Transit District," 1–3.

34. *AC Transit History of Lines by Line: Major Changes since 1960*, July 17, 1978, 7, http://www.actransit.org/wp-content/uploads/History-of-Lines-by-Line.pdf, accessed December 12, 2015.

35. De Leuw, Cather & Company, "Alameda-Contra Costa Transit District," 5.

36. Philip W. Jeffress, "Racial Employment Patterns in the Urban Mass Transportation Industry" (PhD diss., University of Kentucky, 1969), 62; Darold Barnum, "From Private to Public: Labor Relations in Urban Transit," *Industrial and Labor Relations Review* 25, no. 1 (1971): 98.

37. Randal O'Toole, "Urban Transit," 2011, http://www.downsizinggovernment.org/transportation/urban-transit#sthash.r2b3HO8h.dpuf, accessed December 11, 2015.

38. George M. Smerk, *The Federal Role in Urban Mass Transportation* (Bloomington: Indiana University Press, 1991), 101.

39. Cyrius G. Ulberg, *Issues in the Shift from Regional to Local Provision of Bus Service*, Synthesis of Transit Practice 14 (Washington, DC: Transportation Research Board and National Research Council, 1990), 6; George M. Guess, *Public Policy and Transit System Management* (Westport, CT: Greenwood Press, 1990), 9.

40. *AC Transit History of Lines by Line*, 4–6.

41. Robert Nisbet, *From Private to Publicly Owned Transit in the Bay Area: An Oral History Transcript Reflections of the Attorney, Lobbyist, and General Manager of the Alameda Contra Costa Transit District, 1950s to 1980s* (Berkeley: Bancroft Library, University of California–Berkeley, 2004 [Bancroft Collection]): 33 and 53.

42. Ibid., 33, 55.

43. "First Amended Complaint," no. C-74-1859 WHO in the Geraldine Crutchfield, Lucille Jackson, Peggy C. Parker v. AC Transit District, etc., filed November 12, 1974, p. 4; "Interrogatories to Defendant Alameda Contra Costa Transit District," no. C-74-1859 WHO in the Geraldine Crutchfield, Lucille Jackson, Peggy C. Parker v. AC Transit District, etc., filed November 12, 1974.

44. "Consent Decree," no. C-74-1859 WHO in the Geraldine Crutchfield, Lucille Jackson, Peggy C. Parker v. AC Transit District, etc., filed May 29, 1975, pp. 4–5.

45. Ibid., 6.

46. Pate et al. and Van et al., Intervenors v. Alameda Contra Costa Transit District, et al., no. C-76-631 WHO, "Opinion by Judge Orrick for the United States District Court for the Northern District of California," September 28, 1979, p. 13; "Order," no. C-74-1859 WHO in the Geraldine Crutchfield, Lucille Jackson, Peggy C. Parker v. AC Transit District, etc., filed January 12, 1976.

47. AC Transit District, *Transit Times* 19, no. 8 (1977): 7; Gwynn Simpson, "Diversity Training Initiatives: A Synthesis of Transit Practice," in *Transit Cooperative Research Program* (Washington, DC: Transportation Research Board, 2003), 46.

Chapter 3

1. "Affidavit of Donna Pate," filed with the United States District Court for the Northern District of California (1975), 2.

2. Pate et al. and Van et al., Interveners v. Alameda Contra Costa Transit District et al., no C-76-631 WHO, "Opinion by Judge Orrick for the United States District Court Northern District of California," September 28, 1979.

3. Ibid., 24, 13, 17.

4. Ibid., 9, 35.

5. Ibid., 58; Pate, Donna, Kathleen Lewis, and Beverly Lowe v. AC Transit Districts, Alan L. Bingham, and Robert J. Shamoon, United Stated Court of Appeals for the Ninth Circuit (1983), p. 4.

6. Timothy Minchin, "Black Activism, the 1964 Civil Rights Act, and the Racial Integration of the Southern Textile Industry," *The Journal of Southern History* 65, no. 4 (1999): 809–844; Herbert Hill, *Black Labor and the American Legal System* (Washington, DC: Bureau of National Affairs, 1977).

7. "Letter to Mr. Bill McCombe," February 20, 1981, ATU Local 192 from Peter Nussbaum Re: Pate v. A.C. Transit, box 15, 12, pp. 2 and 3, Amalgamated Transit Union, Local 192 Records, Larc.Ms.0327, Labor Archives and Research Center, San Francisco State University (ATU 192 Collection, LARC).

8. Affirmative Action Plan, May 17, 1976, for Crutchfield v. AC Transit, et al., no. C-74-1859 WHO, United States District Court Northern District of California; Leobardo Llamas et al. Complaint, February 9, 1979, Leobardo Llamas et al. v. AC Transit District, no. C-79-0259 WWS, p. 6; Consent Decree, 1979, Leobardo Llamas et al. v. AC Transit District, 10-03-1979, C 79-0259 WHO, p. 4.

9. "Declaration of Peter Nussbaum in Opposition to Motion for Preliminary Injunction," 10-03-1979; Leobardo Llamas et al. v. AC Transit District, C 79-0259 WWS, p. 2; "Memorandum in Support of Plaintiff's Motion to Extend the Consent Decree," 10-9-1983, p. 1; Leobardo Llamas et al. v. AC Transit District, C 79-0259 WWS; Letter to Al Johnson, September 21, 1983, from William J. Flynn Re: Llamas Case, box 15, 23, pp. 1–2, ATU 192 Collection, LARC.

10. Janice Yoder and Patricia Aniakudo, "Outsider within the Firehouse: Subordination and Difference in the Social Interactions of African American Women Firefighters," *Gender & Society* 11 (1997): 324–341; Susan E. Martin, "Outsider within the Station House: The Impact of Race and Gender on Black Women Police," *Social Problems* 41, no. 3 (1994): 383–400; Marion Swerdlow, "Men's Accommodations to Women Entering a Nontraditional Occupation: A Case of Rapid Transit Operatives," *Gender & Society* 3 (1989): 373–381.

11. Swerdlow, "Men's Accommodations to Women Entering a Nontraditional Occupation," 374.

12. Mary Thierry Texeira, "'Who Protects and Serves Me?' A Case Study of Sexual Harassment of African American Women in One U.S. Law Enforcement Agency," *Gender & Society* 16, no. 4 (2002): 524–545.

13. "Operators Injured by Passengers," October 1977, p. 2, box 17, folder 15, ATU 192 Collection, LARC; "1980 Passenger Assaults on Operators," box 17, folder 15, pp. 1 and 7, ATU 192 Collection, LARC.

14. Patti Giuffre and Christine Williams, "Boundary Lines: Labeling Sexual Harassment in Restaurants," *Gender & Society* 8, no. 3 (1994): 378–401.

15. "Complaint for Wrongful Termination," May 11, 2000, Yolanda Jones v. AC Transit, C001679, United States District Court Northern District of California, pp. 2 and 3.

16. Ibid., 4.

17. "Complaint for Violation of F.L.S.A.," July 17, 1991, Rosemary James v. AC Transit, C 91 2190 RHS, United States District Court for the Northern District of California, p. 2.

18. Ibid., 2–3.

19. Ibid., 4.

20. Ibid., 5.

21. "Stipulation and Order for Dismissal," September 3, 1993, Rosemary James v. AC Transit, C-91-2190 RHS, United States District Court Northern District of California.

22. "EEOC Complaint Determination Letter," September 8, 1992, Dorothy Parrish v. AC Transit, Charge no. 376-90-0296, p. 2.

23. "Status Conference Statement," November 5, 1993, Dorothy Parrish v. AC Transit, C-92-4796 EFL, United State District Court Northern District of California, p. 2.

24. "Settlement between Parrish and AC Transit," November 24, 1993; "Employment and Consulting Agreement, Settlement of Litigation, and Mutual General Release," between Dorothy Parrish and AC Transit, p. 4.

25. Benny Evangelista, "AC Transit Official Suspended over Remarks," *The Tribune* (Los Angeles), May 12, 1990, D1-D2, box 18, 22, ATU 192 Collection, LARC; Benny Evangelista, "AC Bus Drivers Threaten Strike Over Racial Slur," *The Tribune* (Los Angeles), May 11, 1990.

26. Evangelista, "AC Bus Drivers Threaten Strike over Racial Slur"; "Houston Buses in Atlanta Experience some Problems," *Houston Chronicle*, August 24, 1996.

27. Dycus v. Amalgamated Transit Union, Local 192, AC Transit, etc., September 7, 1990, "First Amended Complaint for Damages and Request for Injunction," C 901937 JPV, p. 4.

28. "First Amended Complaint," September 10, 1990, Thomas Dycus v. ATU Local 192, AC Transit, Linda Crowe, Charles A. Askin, Williams McCome, James H. Kidd and does 1-10, C-90-1937 JPV, United States District Court Northern District of California; Ely Hill Statement, 1990, exhibit A, Thomas Dycus v. ATU 192 et al., C-90-1937 JPV, United States District Court Northern District of California.

29. "First Amended Complaint," Thomas Dycus v. ATU Local 192, p. 7.

30. AC Transit, "Our 'Stockholders' Write," *Transit Times* 27, no. 7 (1985): 11.

31. Leonard Arbitration, April 22, 1992, "Opinion and Decision of Sam Kagel, arbitrator, Re: Grievance of Leroy Leonard," Sam Kagel Collection, folder 7806,

Labor Archives and Research Center, San Francisco State, University (Sam Kagel Collection, LARC).

32. Ibid., 15.

33. Johnson v. AC Transit, Kelly, 2006, "Plaintiff's Declaration regarding Administrative Hearing Issues," pp. 2 and 9, C 04-04879 MMC, U.S. District Court, Northern District of California.

34. Johnson v. AC Transit, Kelly, 2005, "Deposition of Francois Njike," 04-28-2005, C 04-04879 MMC, U.S. District Court, Northern District of California, p. 62.

35. Ibid., p. 54.

36. Johnson v. AC Transit, Kelly, November 30, 2005, "Plaintiff's Brief about Petition," C 04-04879 MMC, U.S. District Court, Northern District of California.

37. "Opinion by Judge Maxine M. Chesney," February 27, 2006, Johnson v. AC Transit, Kelly, C 04-04879 MMC, U.S. District Court, Northern District of California; "Approved Minutes," October 18, 2006, "Meeting of the AC Transit Retirement Board, GM Memo no. 07-025," p. 2; "Draft Minutes of Special Board of Directors Meeting," January 23, 2008, "AC Transit District," p. 6.

38. Joan R. Acker, "Hierarchies, Jobs, Bodies: A Theory of Gendered Organizations," *Gender & Society* 4, no. 2 (1990): 139–158.

39. James E. Gruber and Lars Bjorn, "Blue-Collar Blues: The Sexual Harassment of Women Autoworkers," *Work and Occupations* 4 (1982): 271–298; Rosabeth Moss Kanter, *Men and Women of the Corporation* (New York: Harper Row, 1977); Suzanne E. Tallichet, "Gender Relations in the Mines and the Division of Labor Underground," *Gender & Society* 9 (1985): 697–711; Sandy Welsh, "Gender and Sexual Harassment," *Annual Review of Sociology* 25 (1999): 169–190.

40. Evelyn Nakano Glenn, "From Servitude to Service Work: Historical Continuities in the Racial Divisions in the Racial Division of Paid Reproductive Labor," *Signs* 18 (1992): 1–43; Cherrie Moraga and Gloria Anzaldœa, eds., *This Bridge Called My Back: Writings by Radical Women of Color* (San Francisco: Kitchen Table/Women of Color Press, 1984); Patricia Hill Collins, "Learning from the Outsider within: The Sociological Significance of Black Feminist Thought," *Social Problems* 33, no. 6 (1986): S14–S32; Yoder and Aniakudo, "Outsider within the Firehouse."

Chapter 4

1. "Union Interview," conducted by Michal F. Settles on October 25, 1990, box 8, folder 15, p. 9, ATU 192 Collection, LARC.

2. Robert E. Nisbet, *From Private to Publicly Owned Transit in the Bay Area: An Oral History Transcript Reflections of the Attorney, Lobbyist, and General Manager of the Alameda Contra Costa Transit District, 1950s to 1980s* (Berkeley: Bancroft Library, University of California–Berkeley, 2004 [Bancroft Collection]).

3. "Union Interview," p. 14.

4. Ibid., 13, 19.

5. "Report on Absenteeism and Attendance Improvement, 1989," Director of Transportation, Sterling Steward's brief review of the Booz, Allen & Hamilton Consultants report commissioned by AC Transit (1989), p. 3, ATU 192 Collection, LARC.

6. Ibid., 1.

7. Ibid., 2.

8. Ibid., 3.

9. Blanche Grosswald, *"I Raised My Kids on the Bus": Transit Shift Workers' Coping Strategies for Parenting* (Berkeley: Center for Working Families, University of California–Berkeley, 1999), 9.

10. Nisbet. *From Private to Publicly Owned Transit in the Bay Area*, 64.

11. Wage data compiled by ATU International illustrates that in 1974, AC Transit's drivers were the highest paid workers in the nation. By 1985, AC Transit operators' ranking among the highest paid operators in the nation declined from fifth to fifteen. See Amalgamated Transit Union International, *Research Department Bulletin* 12 (1985), and *Research Department Bulletin* 1 (1974).

12. *AC Transit Annual Report* (1965/1966): 8; *AC Transit Annual Report* (1980): 7.

13. Frank A. Johnson, *Bus Doctor: From Mechanic to Maintenance Manager at the Alameda-Contra Costa District*, Alameda-Contra Costa Transit District Oral History Series (Berkeley: Bancroft Library, University of California Berkeley Press, 2001), 13–14.

14. Gayland Moffat, Alicia Ashton, and Diane Blackburn, "A Challenged Employment System: Hiring, Training, Performance Evaluation, and Retention of Bus Operators," *TCRP Synthesis* 40 (2001): 10–11.

15. "AC Transit Division 5 Bulletin, N. 2-75." February 19, 1975, box 12, folder 5, ATU 192 Collection, LARC; "Letter to William Lyle by Edward A. Cordeiro," February 19, 1975, box 12, folder 5, ATU 192 Collection, LARC.

16. "Letter to JD Goodman from EA Cordeiro," March 20, 1975 and "Memorandum of Understanding," 1975, Re: Dial-A-Ride-Divisions, Memo between AC Transit & ATU 192, June 1, 1975, box 12, folder 5, ATU 192 Collection, LARC.

17. Concerned Members 192, "Dollars and Sense Breakdown of the January 15th Proposal," box16, folder 8 (1978), ATU 192 Collection, LARC.

18. Mike Libbey, "AC Strikes, the Big Money Loser," *Oakland Tribune*, February 8, 1974; "Strike Ends: Buses are Operating," *Transit Times* 20, no. 7 (Jan. 1978): 4.

19. "Arbitration for Miss Out Policy, Opinion and Decision by William Eaton," January 1, 1975, box 12, folder 22, p. 5, ATU 192 Collection, LARC.

20. Ibid., 6.

21. Ibid., 9.

22. "Letter to Ely Hill Re: Absence Control Arbitration Award," April 8, 1988, box 13, folder 14, ATU 192 Collection, LARC.

23. Ibid., 3.

24. Ibid., 4.

25. "Letter to Arbitration Alexander Cohn, Esq. Re: ACP Award," December 16, 1988, box 13, folder 14, ATU 192 Collection, LARC.

26. "Letter to Peter Nussbaum from Sharon Banks Re: ACP Award," April 17, 1989, box 13, folder 14, ATU 192 Collection, LARC.

27. Ibid., 2.

28. Ibid., 4.

29. Judy Ronnington, "Strike Averted; AC Transit Agrees to Arbitration," *The Tribune* (Los Angeles), September 15, 1989; Alameda County Grand Jury, "Alameda County Grand Jury Final Report: 1988–1989,"Alameda, County of Alameda, California.

30. M. Kompier and V. Di Martino, "Review of Bus Drivers' Occupational Stress and Stress Prevention," *Stress Medicine* 11 (1995): 253–262; Beverly Ann Davenport, "Driving Driven: Urban Transit Operators, Hypertension, and Stress(ed) management" (PhD diss., University of California, San Francisco and Berkeley, 2004); Gary W. Evans and Gunn Johansson, "Urban Bus Driving: An International Arena for the Study of Occupational Health Psychology," *Journal of Occupational Health Psychology* 3, no. 2 (1988): 99–121; Gary W. Evans, "Working on the Hot Seat: Urban Bus Operators," *Accident Analysis and Prevention* 26 (1994): 181–193.

31. D. R Ragland, B. A. Greiner, and J. M. Fisher, "Studies of Health Outcomes in Transit Operators: Policy Implications of Current Scientific Database," *Journal of Occupational Health Psychology* 3 (1998): 172–187; Marilyn Winkleby, "Occupational Stressors and Hypertension Microform: A Study of San Francisco Bus Drivers" (PhD diss., University of California, Berkeley, 1986); Theo Meijman, and Michael Kompier, "Bussy Business: How Urban Bus Drivers Cope with Time Pressure, Passengers, and Traffic Safety," *Journal of Occupational Health Psychology* 3, no. 2 (1998): 99–121.

32. "Union Interview," 3.

33. Kenneth Chomitz, Genevieve Giuliano, and Charles Lane, "Part-Time Operators in Public Transit: Experiences and Prospects," April 1985, Institute of Transportation Studies UCI-ITS-WP-85-3; Kenneth M. Chomitz, *Part-Time Labor, Work Rules, and Transit Costs: Final Report*, Urban Mass Transportation Administration, Office of Policy and Program Development, University Research and Training Division (Springfield, VA: National Technical Information Service, 1981).

34. Grosswald, *"I Raised My Kids on the Bus."*

35. Joram Mayshar and Yoram Halevy, "Shiftwork," *Journal of Labor Economics* 15 (1997): 201; M. J. Colligan and R. R. Rosa, "Shiftwork Effects on Social and Family Life," *Occupational Medicine: State of the Art Reviews* 5 (1990): 315–322.

36. Harriet B. Presser, "Job, Family, and Gender: Determinants of Nonstandard Work Schedules among Employed Americans: 1991," *Demography* 32 (1995): 577–578.

37. Chomitz et al., "Part-Time Operators in Public Transit," 4.

38. Ibid., 17.

39. *Report of AC Transit Employment Activity*, Volumes 54 (1981), 62 (1983), and 66(1985).

40. Chomitz et al., "Part-Time Operators in Public Transit," 15.

41. "Union Interview," 4.

42. "Deficit-Paring Plan: New Budget Targets Internal Savings," *Summer Transit Times* 30 (1988): 4.

43. *AC Transit District Annual Report* (1982): 3.

44. Ibid., 5.

45. AC Transit District, "Memo to Board of Directors," 1987, box 13, folder 10: ATU 192 Collection, LARC.

46. "Brief of Union in Arbitration Proceedings Re: Bus Seat Grievance," November 9, 1987, box 13, folder 10, p. 11, ATU 192 Collection, LARC.

47. "Letter to James Kidd," 1986, Re: Grievance No. M-86-36-Occupational Health and Safety by Edward Billie, April 22, 1986, box 13, file 7, ATU 192 Collection, LARC; "Letter to E. R. Billie," 1987, Re: Anchorlok Seats by Gene Gardiner, August 5, 1987, box 13, file 7, ATU 192 Collection, LARC.

48. "Brief of Union in Arbitration Proceedings Re: Bus Seat Grievance," 2.

49. Ibid., 3.

50. "Lucille Jackson Arbitration," "Opinion and Award by Alexander Cohn, Esq.," November 19, 1987, ATU 192 Records, box 13, file 7, pp. 7–8, ATU 192 Collection, LARC.

51. Ibid. Page 10.

52. "Brief of Union in Arbitration Proceedings Re: Bus Seat Grievance," p. 4.

53. "Letter to James L. O'Sullivan from George Skezas," February 9, 1989, box 13, folder 10, ATU 192 Collection, LARC.

54. AC Transit did have a policy in place since 1974 that excused a woman operator who is unable to work due her physical discomfort while driving. This policy was referred to as the "blue pencil day" because managers used a blue pencil to account for the excused day on the woman driver's attendance card. Although the blue pencil day informally turned into a black pencil day in order to help women avoid teasing from male coworkers in 1981, by 1982, AC Transit decided to get rid of the policy altogether. As such, on December 16, 1981, Transportation Manager Loren A. Ball wrote in A.C.T. no. 136 that "Effective January 1, 1982 cramps (Blue Pencil) will no longer be considered an automatic excuse from work." See "Blue Pencil Day Memo" by Loren A Ball, December 16, 1976, box 9, folder 27, ATU 192 Collection, LARC. Also see "Letter to Robert J. Shamoon, General Manager of AC Transit," December 30, 1981, written by Richard K. Windrich, ATU 192 president–business agent, box 9, folder 27, ATU 192 Collection, LARC.

55. ATU 192 history video, http://www.atu192.org/history/, accessed December 18, 2015.

56. "1983 Contract Proposals," box 8, folder 16, Amalgamated Transit Union, Local 192 Records, Larc.Ms.0327, Labor Archives and Research Center, San Francisco State University.

57. Nicola Dones, "ATU Local 192 and AC Transit Shift into Gear over Work and Family Issues," 2001, CPER No. 147, 12.

58. Ibid., 13.

59. Ibid., 4.

60. California's Wage Order #9 is a regulation passed by the California State Department of Industrial Relations in order to ensure that workers are provided adequate meal and rest periods. While the push for this legislation intensified in 2001, Wage Order #9 took effect July 1, 2004. To read the public hearing transcript documenting transportation union advocacy on this issue throughout the state, see the State of California, Department of Industrial Relations Industrial Welfare Commission, Public Meeting, June 15, 2001, held in San Francisco, California, https://www.dir.ca.gov/iwc/PUBMTG615.htm, accessed May 22, 2015.

61. In section 53 of the 1974, AC Transit first agreed to provide sanitary facilities for transit operators "at each end of the line . . . in order to keep an operator in a healthy situation." The spot time section was added in the 1974 contract wherein the district and ATU 192 agreed how long runs could take and how much time operators would have on both ends of the trip. For instance, the district agreed that operators will have at least eight minutes on each run trip to rest and ten minutes on each end of lengthy runs. Amalgamated Transit Union, Division 192, "Draft of 3/21/74" contract, box 7, folder 11, pp. 39-40, ATU 192 Collection, LARC.

62. "Letter to All Members of Local 192," by Contract Negotiations Committee, April 22, 1977, box 8, folder 2; "1983 Contract Proposals," box 8, folder 16; and "Union Proposal," October 9, 1989, box 13, folder 11, ATU 192 Collection, LARC.

63. "Restroom Availability Issues: Transit and Transportation Drivers," Metroped Feedback from Yvonne W., December 2003, http://americanrestroom .org/pr/transit_op.htm, accessed December 18, 2015.

64. "Contract Agreement between ATU 192 and AC Transit District," effective July 1, 2000, 94, http://www.Dol.gov/olms/regs/compliance/cba/pdf/cbrp0147 .pdf, accessed December 18, 2015.

65. Erik N. Nelson, "AC Transit Drivers: Can't Hold It Any Longer," *Oakland Tribune*, April 2, 2008.

66. "Arbitrator Rules in Favor of Oakland Local in Bathroom Break Dispute," *In Transit; Amalgamated Transit Union AFL-CIO* 120, no. 5 (Sept./Oct. 2011): 29.

67. "Letter to Juan Perez from Edward R. Billie," June 20, 1985, box 13, folder 7, ATU 192 Collection, LARC.

68. "Letter to E. R. Billie from Daniel Ready. Esq.," November 8, 1985, box 9, folder 10, pp. 1-2, ATU 192 Collection, LARC.

69. "Letter to E. L. Cota et al. from Alan Kopke, Esq.," August 31, 1985, box 9, folder 10, ATU 192 Collection, LARC.

70. Ibid., 3.

71. "Letter to Richard Windrich," 1980, Re: Access Litigation by Peter Nussbaum, Esq., February 25, 1980, box 15, file 7, ATU 192 Collection, LARC.

72. Ibid., 2.

73. ATU 192 history video.

74. Amalgamated Transit Union, Division 192, "Draft of 3/21/74" contract, 20-24.

75. Ibid., 29.

76. "Letter to Mr. Rodriguez from I. P. Cordeiro," November 25, 1981, box 16, folder 19, ATU 192 Collection, LARC.

77. "Complaint for Declaratory Relief" no. 591944-8, Gene Wright v. Local Division 192, Amalgamated Transit Union, etc., box 15, ATU 192 Collection, LARC.

78. Alameda County Grand Jury, "Alameda County Grand Jury Final Report."

Chapter 5

1. "2 Investigates: Drivers Ticketed for Stopping at BART Station Curb for Just Seconds," http://wjbk.dua1.worldnow.com/story/27055096/2-investigates-drivers -ticketed-for-stopping-at-bart-station-curb-for-just-seconds, accessed December 18, 2015.

2. Joe Ward, "Bus Driver Involved in Attack to Return to Work," *Kenosha News*, February 21, 2014,http://www.kenoshanews.com/news/bus_driver_involved_in _attack_to_return_to_work_475755059.html, accessed December 18, 2015; Martine Powers, "MBTA Tightens No-Phone Policy for Drivers," *Boston Globe*, June 16, 2014, http://www.bostonglobe.com/2014/06/16/mbta-announces-stricter-policy -for-cellphone-possession-workers-wake-newton-bus-crash/Y6vIdwWn VLXP9mvjpmO6FI/story.html, accessed December 18, 2015; Ashley Rodriguez Share, "CATS Drivers Complain of Unfair Punishments," May 18, 2010, News Source: WBRZ, http://www.wbrz.com/mobile/story.cfm?n=10415, accessed December 18, 2015; "New York, Transit Union at Odds over Wages, Discipline," New York Times News Service, December 11, 1999, http://articles.baltimoresun.com/1999 -12-11/news/9912110126_1_infractions-disciplinary-procedures-york-city, accessed December 18, 2015.

3. Janice Yoder and Patricia Aniakudo, "Outsider within the Firehouse: Subordination and Difference in the Social Interactions of African American Women Firefighters," *Gender & Society* 11 (1997): 324–341.

4. Reba Gauer, *Straight Run: Oral History Transcript: Thirty-Nine Years Driving a Bus for the AC Transit District*, Alameda-Contra Costa Transit District Oral History Series (Bancroft: University of California Press, 2003), 25.

5. Transcript of Hearing, 1980, Re: Johnny C. Jackson, October 20, 1980, box 13, file 2, ATU 192 Collection, LARC.

6. Ibid., 8.

7. Ibid., 3.

8. Ibid., 19.

9. Ibid., 24.

10. Ibid., 25.

11. "Letter to Loren A. Ball, Transportation Manager," May 10, 1983, box 9, folder 47, ATU 192 Collection, LARC.

12. Turner Arbitration, "Opinion and Award of the Board of Arbitration, by Adolph M. Koven, Esq.," January 20, 1984, ATU 192 Collection, LARC.

13. Ibid., 3.

14. Ibid., 10.

15. John R. Riley, Administrator, Federal Railroad Administration Statement before the Senate Judiciary Committee, April 9, 1987.

16. U.S. Congress, *Drug Testing in the Workplace. Hearings before Committee on the Judiciary, United States Senate, 100th Congress*, 1st sess, Senate Committee on the Judiciary, April 19 and May 13, 1987, p. 15.

17. Ibid., 23.

18. Associated Press, "Negligence Cited in Amtrak Crash: Conrail Engineer Indicted on Manslaughter Charges," *Los Angeles Times*, May 5, 1987; Associated Press "Figure in Railroad Drug Tests Guilty on 3 Counts," *Houston Chronicle*, May 26, 1987, sec. 1,5; Associated Press, "Researcher Resigns U.S. Post after Performing Fake Tests," *New York Times*, June 13, 1987.

19. U.S. Congress, *Drug Testing in the Workplace*, 58.

20. Ibid., 57.

21. Ibid., 159.

22. Spears Arbitration, "Opinion and Decision of the Board of Arbitration by Barbara Bridgewater, J. D. Re: Discharge of Anthony Spears," March 19, 1979, box 14, file 4, p. 24, ATU 192 Collection, LARC.

23. Wilson Arbitration, "Opinion and Decision of the Board of Arbitration by Barbara Bridgewater, J. D. Re: Discharge of P. J. Wilson," July 24, 1980, p. 17, ATU 192 Collection, LARC.

24. Ibid., 25.

25. Ibid., 8.

26. Wallace Arbitration, "Opinion and Decision of the Board of Arbitration by William Eaton, Arbitration, Re; Discharge of Clawson Wallace," July 26, 1975, box 14, file 4, ATU 192 Collection, LARC.

27. Ibid., 1.

28. Ibid., 3.

29. Johnson Arbitration, "Opinion and Decision of the Board of Arbitration by Geraldine M. Randall, Arbitration Re: Discharge of Bernice E. Johnson," October 19, 1979, ATU 192 Collection, LARC.

30. Ibid., 5.

31. Ibid., 6.

32. Ibid., 7.

33. Ibid., 6.

34. Ibid., 12.

35. Ibid., 7.

36. Ibid., 13.

37. ATU 192 referenced the Allen Arbitration wherein the arbitrator reversed AC Transit's decision to discharge the transit operator because he found no just cause for the discipline. The district only could establish that, since Allen consumed two glasses of wine at lunch at 1 P.M. and 4 P.M., his breath smelled like alcohol. The arbitrator ruled that since he smelled like alcohol, he committed a minor violation of the district's rule; at the same time, the arbitrator found that a discharge was too severe for an arbitrary violation. In turn, Allen was reinstated.

38. Ibid., 15–16.

39. Ibid., 8 and 12.

40. Ibid., 22–24.

41. Ibid., 31–35.

42. "Letter to Richard E. Windrich from Wayne Onizuka," Re: Blood or urine specimen collection, August 1, 1979, box16, folder 11, ATU 192 Collection, LARC.

43. "Margaret Hayes Arbitration Opinion and Award," December 27, 1989, box 16, folder 11, ATU 192 Collection, LARC.

44. Ibid., 5.

45. Ibid., 3–4.

46. Ibid., 7.

47. Ibid., 6, 7, 10.

48. Judy Ronningen, "Random Drug Tests to Begin for Transit Workers," *Oakland Tribune*, December 3, 1989, A-1 and A-4; Judy Ronningen, "Transit Operators, Riders Both Divided on Drug Test Issue," *Oakland Tribune*, December 3, 1989, A5.

49. Lennart E. Henriksson, "Consequences of Drug Testing Programs in Urban Mass Transit" (PhD diss., Indiana University, 1991), 18.

50. Ibid., 11.

51. Ibid., 18.

52. Ibid., 26.

53. Federal Transit Administration, "FTA Substance Abuse Management Oversight Audit Report, 1999," FTA Recipient: Alameda-Contra Costa Transit District, Corrective Action Date Reports for Selected Random Tests: February 19, 1999, November 15, 1999, October 6, 1999, January 26, 2000, March, 13, 2000, pursuant to FOIA Request to US Department of Transportation, Federal Transit Administration, file no. 10-0149 (FTA FOIA Records).

54. Federal Transit Administration, "FTA Substance Abuse Management Oversight Audit Report," February 19, 1999, November 12, 1999, and November 15, 1999, 6.

55. Ibid., 6–12.

56. Ibid., 18.

57. Ibid., 20.

58. Ibid., 102.

59. Ibid., 21–23.

60. Ibid., 25.

61. Ibid., 74 and 77.

62. Ibid., 34 and 57.

63. Ibid., 34–36.

64. Federal Transit Administration. "FTA Substance Abuse Management Oversight Audit Report," February 25, 2002, 3 and 5.

65. Federal Transit Administration, "FTA Substance Abuse Management Oversight Audit Report, 1999," February 19, 1999, November 15, 1999, October 6, 1999, January 26, 2000, March, 13, 2000), 36, 69–72.

66. Tyler Hartwell, Paul Steele, Michael French, and Nathaniel Rodman, "Prevalence of Drug Testing in the Workplace," *Monthly Labor Review Online* 118, no. 11 (Nov. 1996): 36–37.

67. Kenneth D. Tunnell, *Pissing on Demand: Workplace Drug Testing and the Rise of the Detox Industry* (New York: New York University Press, 2004), 18, 54; Thomas E. Backer and Kirk B. O'Hara, *Organizational Change and Drug-Free Workplaces: Templates for Success* (Westport, CT: Quorum Books, 1991), 25.

68. Tunnell, *Pissing on Demand*; Hartwell et al., "Prevalence of Drug Testing in the Workplace," 36–61; Michael R. O'Donnell, "Employee Drug Testing—Balancing the Interests in the Workplace: A Reasonable Suspicion Standard," *Virginia Law Review* 74 (1988): 969–1009.

Chapter 6

1. Barbara Reskin and Patricia Roos, *Job Queues, Gender Queues: Explaining Women's Inroads into Male Occupations* (Philadelphia: Temple University, 1990); Marlese Durr and John R. Logan, "Racial Submarkets in Government Employment: African American Managers in New York State," *Sociological Forum* 12, no. 3 (1997): 353–370; Evelyn Nakano Glenn, *Unequal Freedom: How Race and Gender Shaped American Citizenship and Labor* (Cambridge, MA: Harvard University Press, 2002).

2. "Union Interview," conducted by Michal F. Settles on October 25, 1990, box 8, folder 15, pp. 26–27, ATU 192 Collection, LARC.

3. Ibid., 34.

4. Beverly Ann Davenport, "Driving Driven: Urban Transit Operators, Hypertension, and Stress(ed) Management" (PhD diss, University of California, San Francisco and Berkeley, 2004); G. Aronsson and A. Rissler, "Psychophysiological Stress Reactions in Female and Male Urban Bus Drivers," *Journal of Occupational Health Psychology* 3 (1998): 122–129; Robert E. Spicher, "Review of Literature Related to Bus Operator Stress," in *Research Results Digest* National Cooperative Transit Research & Development Program. (Washington, DC: National Research Council, 1982).

5. S. M. Stanley, H. J. Markman, M. St. Peters, and B. Leber, "Strengthening Marriages and Preventing Divorce: New Directions in Prevention Research," *Family Relations* 44 (1995): 392–401; Jeffry H. Larson, Stephan M. Wilson, and Rochelle Beley, "The Impact of Job Insecurity on Marital and Family Relationships," *Family Relations* 43, no. 2 (April 1994): 138–143; Ann C. Crouter and Beth Manke, "The Changing American Workplace: Implications for Individuals and Families," *Family Relations* 43, no. 2 (1994): 117–124.

6. Puck Lo and Marcy Rein, "San Francisco Bay Area Transit Justice Movement Emerges," *Race, Poverty & the Environment* 17, no. 2 (2010): 45–52.

7. Darrick Hamilton, Algeron Austin, and William Darity Jr., "Whiter Jobs, Higher Wages: Occupational Segregation and the Lower Wages of Black Men," EPI Briefing Paper 288 (Washington, DC: Economic Policy Institute, 2011).

8. Guillermo Mayer and Richard A. Marcantonio, "Bay Area Transit—Separate and Unequal," *Race, Poverty & Environment* 17, no. 1 (2010): 31.

9. Ibid., 30.

10. Lo and Rein, "San Francisco Bay Area Transit Justice Movement Emerges," 47.

11. Mayer and Marcantonio, "Bay Area Transit—Separate and Unequal."

12. Lo and Rein, "San Francisco Bay Area Transit Justice Movement Emerges," 48.

13. Steven Pitts, "Transit Unions: Key Allies in the Struggle for Transportation Justice," *Race, Poverty & Environment* 12, no. 1 (2006): 68–69; Luz D. Cervantes, "Transit Workers and Environmentalists Join Forces," *Race, Poverty & Environment* 17, no. 1 (2010): 40–41; Geoff Ray, "LA Bus Riders' Union Rolls over Transit Racism," *Race, Poverty & Environment* 12, no. 1 (2006): 54–55.

Index

San Francisco, 33–34, 40–41, 48–49,
155–156
San Francisco Muni, 98
Seniority system, 10, 19, 144; Seniority
rights, 11, 24, 91, 97, 101, 104–105
Sex discrimination, 20, 124. *See also*
AC Transit
Sick leave, 10, 68–69, 80–81, 87,
95–96, 99, 146
South California Transit District, 53
Southern Pacific Company, 40–41
Split shifts, 2, 6–7, 85–86, 91, 98, 100,
146
Straight through runs, 100, 146
Substance abuse, 111, 117–119, 121, 127,
131–132, 136, 174. *See also* Marijuana

Taft-Hartley Act, 46
Transit industry, 6–7, 9, 35, 40–42,
47–50, 117, 161, 163
Transportation industry, 34, 119; 164.
See also Transit industry
Two-tiered, 10, 11, 145; Two-Tiered
Employment Relations, 145

TWU (Transport Workers Union),
24, 111, 119, 128

UMTA (Urban Mass Transportation
Administration), 52, 58, 127–128, 152
Unemployment, 4, 7, 39, 143
Union Pacific Railroad accident, 118

War Labor Board, 37
War Manpower Commission, 30, 42,
45–46, 163
Welfare, 8–9, 25, 85, 144, 160–161
WestCAT (Western Contra Costa
Transit Authority), 1–2
West Oakland, 38–39, 110
Windrich, Richard K., 106, 125,
170–171, 174
Work conditions, 3, 12, 33, 139; Work
policies, 22; Work process, 100,
144–145; Work rules, 11, 84, 103,
141–143, 150; Work/life conflicts,
2–3, 33, 81, 83–84, 97, 107, 148
Work/life imbalances, 15, 79. *See also*
Work conditions

CPSIA information can be obtained
at www.ICGtesting.com
Printed in the USA
BVHW030911131218
535331BV00030B/374/P